ar

G000124079

a guide to contemporary art spaces

•••

martin coomer
photographs by keith collie and heike löwenstein

art london

a guide to contemporary art spaces

• • • **ellipsis**

•••

BRITISH LIBRARY CATALOGUING IN PUBLICATION
A CIP record for this book is available from the British Library

PUBLISHED BY •••ellipsis
2 Rufus Street London N1 6PE
E MAIL ...@ellipsis.co.uk
www http://www.ellipsis.com
SERIES EDITOR Tom Neville
SERIES DESIGN Jonathan Moberly

COPYRIGHT © 1999 Ellipsis London Limited
ISBN 1 899858 75 X

FILM PROCESSING METRO IMAGING

PRINTING AND BINDING Hong Kong

•••ellipsis is a trademark of Ellipsis
London Limited

For a copy of the Ellipsis catalogue or
information on special quantity orders
of Ellipsis books please contact
Lindsay Evans
0171–739 3157 or lindsay@ellipsis.co.uk

art london: a guide to contemporary art spaces

Martin Coomer 1999

contents

0 introduction
1 east end
2 old street/shoreditch
3 clerkenwell
4 warren street area
5 cork street area
6 dering street
7 frith street/covent garden
8 the rest of w1
9 north london
10 west london
11 notting hill
12 sw1
13 se1
14 south london
15 index
16 index of artists

Introduction

This book contains descriptions of 60 gallery spaces in London, focusing on the best contemporary art the capital has to offer. It by no means includes all galleries or represents all points of view, but the selection spotlights those spaces crucial to the phenomenal interest in British art that has developed during the 1990s, and those that will ensure its place in public consciousness well into the next century. With round-ups of key exhibitions of recent years plus those planned for the next, it is a geographic guide to the vast array of art being produced and shown in the capital, and one that should be as useful to the connoisseur as it is to the uninitiated or simply curious.

Though his pursuits now seem to rest with dubious pop records, the go-getting attitude of Damien Hirst and his Goldsmiths' College contemporaries has left a legacy of confidence and ambition. Seminal shows of the late 1980s such as *Freeze*, held in a disused Docklands warehouse, spawned not only the careers of Fiona Rae, Ian Davenport, Hirst and Gary Hume, but also hundreds of imitators. The property slump at the beginning of the 1990s enabled artists to open spaces which were not reliant on funding. As West-End commercial galleries folded and few apart from Charles Saatchi were buying art, young artists gained freedom to make the kind of work they chose – often irreverent, sometimes ephemeral, usually cheap to produce – and had people driving to the East End in droves. Those galleries that survived couldn't fail to take note, especially as these makeshift spaces, in the East End and around Old Street in particular, became the most fashionable in town. Most of the Hirst generation are now represented by established West-End galleries but for young artists there is still no art market to speak of, so their work often takes the form of pseudo commodities, conceptual one-liners and visual puns.

And London has more so-called alternative spaces than ever. They seem to crop up overnight and often disappear as quickly. Most are still concentrated around the East End, which remains the most accurate barometer of the contemporary-art scene – not least because it is where most young artists live, or at least rent studios, and from where ideas and trends filter out. Cheap rents enable the truly alternative to turn unexpected places into salons, semi-permanent spaces or venues for one-off events. The East End is not high on glamour, but it is where networks of strong friendships among young artists exist and where life, to a large extent, is governed by the private view and the pub round the corner. Whitechapel, Bow and, to the north, Hackney boast many of the best commercial, alternative and non-profit-making public spaces in town. On their doorstep, but with a decidedly different flavour, are the streets around Old Street and Hoxton Square, once considered a backwater, now home to ultra-cool warehouse dwellers, design studios and galleries. Gentrification of the area may have made rents prohibitively high but, somehow, new spaces continue to open.

Moving south, Deptford High Street is the unlikely location for two of London's more ambitious spaces – Hales Gallery and the Museum of Installation. Beaconsfield and Milch in Vauxhall and Delfina Studios and Gallery in Bermondsey Street, close to London Bridge Station, attest to the strength of south London. Even north London, something of a wilderness, compensates for its dearth of decent spaces with the magnificent Saatchi Gallery – a private gallery that is regarded as a public museum. Cork Street and its surrounding area – the traditional stronghold of London's commercially run spaces which during the economic crash became all but deserted – are once again flourishing with Asprey Jacques, Entwistle and Stephen Friedman joining Victoria Miro, who staved off the recession, and Waddington Galleries, who tested the water with painters

Introduction

Fiona Rae and Ian Davenport from the Hirst generation but seems reluctant to embrace fully the wave of young stars who have since emerged.

All of this augurs well for the continued health of the scene. But to say that British art is thriving still seems tantamount to tempting fate. The visual arts in this country are severely underfunded, our institutions too crippled or cautious to respond to the latest developments. Art in general is given a rough ride by the British media, so much so that acceptance and widespread promotion is anathema to its spirit. More than this, it seems terribly un-British. A hop across the English Channel to the well-funded colleges and institutions of the continent reveals the relatively lacklustre result of having little to kick against. Tapping into the psyche of our class-ridden society unleashes a healthy two-fingered salute at the establishment. The more blatant gestures continue to goad the philistine press. But, as such, the contemporary art scene is held in a fragile balance. Until now, it has been precisely the things that have held young artists back that have fuelled them. Tony Blair's embrace of 'Cool Britannia' and countless analogies with Brit Pop and with the swinging London of the 1960s evoke images of a mythical land of Mini Coopers, meat pies and smoky pubs – all good for the nation's invisible earnings but a far cry from reality and from the real creative energy that buzzes around the city.

The London art scene is, above all, constantly evolving. Still hard up for the most part, it is a diffident and difficult creature and more exciting for it. The *Sensation* exhibition at the Royal Academy in 1997, regardless of the column inches and public debate, saw the entry of our bad boys and girls into the establishment and in its wake the art scene seems more varied, less settled than ever. Gallerists and collectors jostle to find the next big thing, when there probably isn't one. We even have a new -ism – 'New Neurotic Realism' – packaged and presented by Charles Saatchi.

The truth is more complicated. As this book shows, there is no one type of art being produced, and certainly no dominant movement, just good and bad, as in any generation. Painting, sculpture, video, installation – nothing holds sway, and the roles of artist, critic and curator are no longer set in stone.

This book is a selective guide to where you might find the best contemporary art in the capital. Notable omissions include the Marlborough Gallery and the Bernard Jacobson Gallery, both of which have been important, and the Royal Academy, which presented *Sensation* in 1997 but whose lasting contribution to contemporary art is the hateful annual *Summer Exhibition*. The Tate Gallery is, in this edition, represented solely by its Art Now room, a project space that consistently shows work by young artists. Hopelessly inadequate, it highlights the need for the Tate Gallery of Modern Art at Bankside, which is due to open in the year 2000.

Those that I would love to have featured include City Racing, the artist-run gallery in Vauxhall which, during the decade before its closure in December 1998, staged more than 50 shows by luminaries such as Sarah Lucas, Gillian Wearing, Mark Wallinger, and Mat Collishaw, and Cabinet Gallery, the tiny Brixton mansion flat from where Martin McGowan brought us the best of young British and, in particular, American artists, which looks set to move to the Clerkenwell area in 1999.

ACKNOWLEDGEMENTS
Thank you to all the galleries and individuals who have been so supportive of this project, especially to those whose ears have been consistently bent by my requests for information. For more patience than I thought possible, I owe Tom Neville and all at ellipsis a huge debt of gratitude.
MC January 1999

art london: a guide to contemporary art spaces

east end

Whitechapel Art Gallery	1.2
One in the Other	1.6
The Nunnery	1.8
Matt's Gallery	1.10
Chisenhale Gallery	1.16
Camerawork	1.20
The Approach	1.22
The Showroom	1.24
Anthony Wilkinson Fine Art	1.28
Interim Art	1.30
Flowers East	1.32
Paton Gallery	1.34

Whitechapel Art Gallery

Designed at the turn of the century in the arts and crafts style by Charles Harrison Townsend, the Whitechapel, like the South London Gallery (see page 14.8), was built to bring art to the underprivileged local community. Tower Hamlets is still one of the country's poorest boroughs but it can boast a flagship exhibition space that has housed such celebrated exhibits as Picasso's 'Guernica', now on permanent display at the Gallery Reina Sofia in Madrid, and held landmark exhibitions of key artists throughout the century. Today it is an independent space, a registered charity that receives half its income from public sources including the Arts Council, and finds an annual £500,000 from commercial sponsors, trusts and individual patrons. The galleries were last modernised in 1998 and are complemented by a café, a bookshop run by Zwemmer, a lecture theatre and an education room. Part of the education programme has been an on-going collaboration with the schools and colleges of the borough.

Solo shows by prominent and influential international artists have been among the most memorable of recent years. Included in the 1996 programme were the beautiful, cinematic images of Jeff Wall, and Bill Viola's emotionally intense video works. 1998 kicked off with a fantastic mid-career retrospective of Thomas Schütte who, with unsettling discrepancies in scale and pace and with astonishing breadth, presents us with all the problems of being in the world, of reacting with or responding to others. His daft metal humanoid 'Grosse Geisters' (Big Spirits) were complemented by 'United Enemies', small caricatures pinched and worried from Fimo and bound in pairs or trios by bits of cloth. In the upstairs gallery was a melancholy street of architectural models and drawings that owe something to the harsh light and menace of de Chirico, something to utopian designs for living, with all the dashed hopes and false promises they now stand for. In July Peter Doig's second solo exhi-

Whitechapel Art Gallery

bition at the gallery was followed by the group show *Speed* curated by Jeremy Millar. Contrary to the publicity, *Speed* wasn't a bullet-train ride through the century's countless technological revolutions, but an old-style museum show that seemed wilfully to admit that our relationship with speed is far more complex than a bunch of static objects could ever demonstrate. Some exhibits, Richard Hamilton's 'Hommage à Chrysler Corp' of 1957 for example, were sexy and glamorous and full of optimism; others, including John Minton's 'Composition: The Death of James Dean', were poignant reminders of the destructive force of speed.

The biennial *Whitechapel Open*, held here and at various other local venues, invites submissions from the thousands of artists who live in the East End. But inevitably, with its one-work-per-artist policy, it fails to be the blue-riband event it ought. The problem is in part to do with how the gallery views its role. Pandering to a notion of community spirit, it remains as inclusive as possible, while highlighting the fact that a 'something for everyone' policy does no one any real favours. Notable entrants in 1998, however, were Daniel Coombs, Gary Simmonds and Jerwood-Painting-Prize-winner Madeleine Strindberg.

The 1998/99 programme features solo shows by Rosemary Trockel and Terry Winters, a *Young Internationals* group show of significant young painters from around the globe, and a month of programming encompassing Asian art, fashion, film and music. In 2001 the Whitechapel will celebrate its centenary and to commemorate will publish a book revisiting many of its major exhibitions.

ADDRESS Whitechapel High Street, London E1 7QX (0171-522 7888)
OPEN Tuesday to Sunday 11.00–17.00, Wednesday until 20.00
TUBE Aldgate East BUS 25, 67, 253

One in the Other

This diminutive low-key space is situated on the first floor of a Victorian warehouse, off the beaten track of the so-called new bohemia though a stone's throw away from Brick Lane and Shoreditch. What One in the Other lacks in size it makes up for in integrity, showing sparse but carefully selected exhibitions that have featured paintings by Alessandro Raho and drawings by Claude Heath. Mark Titchner's July 1998 show included kinetic sculptures that, while not exactly breaking the late-1990s' lad-art mould, offer more than one might imagine. Mixing back-bedroom electronics with a sprinkling of sci-fi in a variety of clumsy forms, he adds poetic resonance to the Blue-Peter bodge job. Visitors entered between two inverted cones, each housing a speaker and a dish of coloured water. Sounds, like the rumblings of a Massive Attack intro, reverberated inside each podium, agitating the dark liquid which danced – sometimes like distressed silk, sometimes miraculously still – to the changing frequency.

In September Leo de Goede showed just one painting of elliptical shapes, like wood grain gone psychedelic, which references both the colour-field paintings of Clyfford Still and computer-imaging techniques. *2in1(x4+1)*, a group show including Gary Perkins, 1998 artist in residence at the Liverpool Tate, and Kate Belton, known for her photographs of tiny mock-ups of rooms, rounded off the year.

ADDRESS 1 Tenter Ground, London E1 7NH (0171–564 8282)
OPEN Saturday and Sunday 12.00–18.00
TUBE Liverpool Street BUS 8, 26, 35, 48, 78, 149, 242

The Nunnery

One of several studio complexes in the capital with attached gallery, Bow Arts Trust occupies two large buildings on the north side of Bow Road opposite St Mary Atta le Bow Church, of the famous Bow Bell. A non-profit making-institution, funded initially by artists from the Trust and private sponsors, The Nunnery comprises two impressive gallery spaces linked by a tiled corridor in the former convent. Since summer 1998 the programme has comprised two group shows of artists resident in the studios, and *Alice,* a touring exhibition which examines the myth of child-hood as a time of purity and innocence and includes Machiko Edmondson's photorealist portrait of a baby, Lucy Wood's glass and steel reconstruction of a playground roundabout, and photo-text works by Tracey Moffatt.

The 1999/2000 programme includes *Aurifiction and Aurifaction,* a group show including Torie Begg and Rachel Chapman, a solo show of Nicky Hobermann's kooky paintings of children, and an installation by John Frankland, whose mock-up of a corporate foyer has been a semi-permanent installation at the Saatchi Gallery.

Reflecting the degree of professionalism now shown by many artist-run spaces, The Nunnery complements its exhibitions with an education programme funded by the National Lottery, has set up a web site and is exploring ways of raising revenue through a magazine and café.

ADDRESS 183 Bow Road, London E3 2SJ (0181–980 7774)
OPEN Thursday to Sunday 11.00–18.00
TUBE Bow Road BUS S2, 8, 25

Matt's Gallery

Few galleries have maintained a reputation for experimentation for as long as Matt's. For almost two decades, under the careful guidance of director Robin Klassnik, Matt's has provided the time, space and, crucially, the funds for artists to make and show work that other venues would be unable or unwilling to accommodate. Klassnik, who trained as a painter and had some success with his own photographic/text work, started the gallery in 1979 in Martello Street, near London Fields, long before the area became the art-world magnet it is today. Matt's is possibly the only gallery to have been named after a dog – Klassnik's Old English sheepdog Matt E Mulsion.

For many years Klassnik subsidised the gallery solely by his teaching career. With grant assistance, he was able gradually to give up full-time teaching and in 1992 Matt's moved to its current address, a warehouse space in Copperfield Road, Bow, which is also home to ACME artists studio headquarters, close to Mile End tube station and within walking distance of Chisenhale (see page 1.16).

Matt's is still a labour of love. Non-profit making, though it does now represent artists and has sold its fair share of work to both the Tate Gallery and Saatchi collections, it is reliant upon public funding and run by a skeleton staff. Matt's has proved to be one of the most malleable galleries in town; to incorporate what have become some of the most important site-specific works of the last two decades, significant alterations to the infrastructure have had to be made.

Richard Wilson's installation '20 50', the expanse of sump oil that has been on permanent display at the Saatchi Gallery since 1987, was initially created for Matt's. Wilson has also disrupted the gallery space by cutting out the window frames, tilting them into the gallery to create spatial conundrums ('She Came in Through the Bathroom Window', 1989) and

digging down to the water table deep beneath the gallery, covering the trench with a billiard table fitted flush to the floor and inserting a cement pipe in one corner. ('Watertable', 1994). Others to tamper with the architecture include Melanie Counsell, who in 1995 added a false ceiling that extended almost to the windows where sheets of black Perspex reflected the light from outside. It looked almost nothing, but with the changing light, the gallery itself became a canvas of shifting mood and atmosphere.

Established artists such as Avis Newman, Tony Bevan and Willie Doherty have been able to create large works specially for the space. Bevan spent 18 months making his enormous charcoal 'painting' of a single recumbent head and, so that it could be viewed without the gallery pillars obscuring its 6-metre span, a new wall had to be built. Doherty, who sites his work in the troubled territory of Northern Ireland, was shortlisted for the 1994 Turner Prize and, in the same year was awarded the Glen Dimplex Award for 'The Only Good One is a Dead One', a double-screen video installation originally commissioned by Matt's. The two videos were shot in nighttime Derry – one from a parked car, the other from a car travelling down a winding country road – and are accompanied by a soundtrack of an Irish male voice who imagines being both victim and perpetrator of terrorist violence. Fluctuating between fear and fantasy, the installation sidesteps the media tendency to polarise, to create a 'them-and-us' scenario, and instead points towards a wider, more ambiguous reading of conflict.

Klassnik's generosity of spirit also extends to younger artists, some fresh from college, who are offered the important step of solo shows early in their careers. Xenia Dieroff showed her video installation 'Involuntary Confessions', a series of short films that explored the ambiguities of facial expression, in December 1996, shortly after leaving Gold-

Matt's Gallery

smiths' College. In June 1998, young Scottish artist Graham Fagen presented 'Peek-a-Jobby', a sculptural installation reminiscent of a theatre set and a booklet of a script set in the room, with a bizarre and faintly disturbing conclusion.

Signalling the gallery's twentieth-anniversary year in 1999, Matt's presented *Backspace*, a three-month-long project bringing together documentary information and artworks in one gallery and a programme of week-long exhibitions of new work by artists associated with the gallery in the other space.

ADDRESS 42–44 Copperfield Road, London E3 4RR (0181-983 1771)
OPEN Wednesday to Sunday 12.00–18.00
TUBE Mile End BUS D6, 25, 277

Chisenhale Gallery

A former veneer factory, tucked away in an otherwise residential East End street, Chisenhale contains a dance space, artists' studios and a 250-square-metre gallery which has shown its mettle exhibiting sculpture, installation and, in particular, video and film. With no natural light, the space can prove somewhat daunting to painters; however, Lisa Milroy and French artist Bernard Frize, who exhibited his smart and insouciant 'Suite a Rollo' series in 1994, both managed to enliven what is often described as a bunker.

Set up by artists in 1986, Chisenhale is now an independent publicly financed gallery, a registered charity which receives revenue funding from the London Arts Board and assistance with its educational programme the from the London Borough of Tower Hamlets. The gallery famously gave Rachel Whiteread her first one-person show and is a stone's throw away from the site of 'House', the cast of the interior of a late nineteenth-century terraced house in Grove Road, which won her the 1993 Turner Prize and might have stood as one of the greatest public sculptures in this country but was subsequently demolished.

Chisenhale bears testimony to the strength of women artists over the last decade. Cornelia Parker, nominated for the Turner Prize in 1997, exhibited 'Cold Dark Matter', the charred remnants of a shed exploded for her by the army. Recent director Judith Nesbitt kicked off an ambitious programme with Swiss artist Pipilotti Rist, whose video installation 'Slept in, had a bath, highly motivated' was a surreal blend of cut-and-paste short films heavily influenced by her background in pop promos. Gillian Wearing showed '10-16', her film of adults miming to the voices of children here, and 1998 Turner-Prize-nominee Sam Taylor-Wood presented 'Pent-Up', five cinematic vignettes in which the monologues of crisis-ridden characters collided in the darkened space.

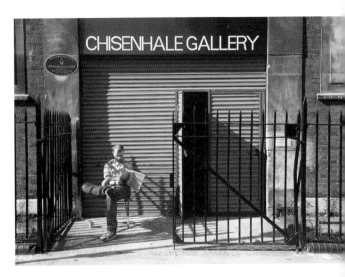

Chisenhale Gallery

For a space reliant on funding, Chisenhale has managed to attract the biggest names while retaining a reputation for off-beat shows, like *Don't Hate, Sculpt* by Bob and Roberta Smith (aka Patrick Brill), and 'Hertford Union' by Simon Faithfull, who diverted the nearby canal into the gallery through a series of pipes and bottles. Events such as *Turning the Tables*, in which guests such as Interim Art director Maureen Paley and *Time Out*'s Sarah Kent were invited to DJ for the evening, and *NWUK*, a run of one-week shows in summer 1998, selected from open submission, spice up the regular programme.

ADDRESS 64 Chisenhale Road, London E3 5QZ (0181–981 4518)
OPEN Wednesday to Sunday 13.00–18.00
TUBE Mile End BUS D6, 8, 277

Camerawork

Recently reopened, Camerawork looks set to build on its 20-year reputation as a focal point for lens-based work. The rather 1980s-looking building, surely the only gallery with an automatic sliding door, provides darkroom facilities and a gallery space which, under the guidance of recent director John Roberts, has kept abreast of latest developments, adding gravitas to the programme with historical surveys. In 1997 'The Impossible Document' looked at the link between British photography and early conceptual art, using examples by Art & Language, Victor Burgin, John Hilliard, and John Stezaker. *Pals and Chums*, also in 1997, took a more popular-culture route, looking at young British artists dealing with fact, fiction and photographic 'truth'.

The latest technology was used by Max Fenton, with the aid of Justin Owen, whose credits include special effects on *Mission: Impossible*, in his installation 'Sublimer'. On one wall Fenton hung a huge photograph of the mirror image of the gallery interior, projecting on to it computer-manipulated video images of a white figure who seemed to walk into the image. Flashy but not terribly successful, it highlights a tendency among some artists to gorge on the latest developments without transforming them into anything other than mute spectacle. Better was Rod Dickinson's rather beautiful photographic survey of crop circles of April 1998, shown shortly before the temporary closure of the gallery.

ADDRESS 121 Roman Road, London E2 0QN (0181–980 6256)
OPEN Monday to Saturday 13.00–18.00, Sunday 12.00–17.00
TUBE Bethnal Green BUS D6, 8, 106, 253

The Approach

Since opening in March 1997, The Approach has eclipsed most alternative East End venues. The 800-square-foot space – a former function room above a Bethnal Green pub – set its agenda of promoting high-quality contemporary art with a group show of painters Dan Sturgis and Liz Arnold and sculptor Jane Simpson, all of whom have been collected by Charles Saatchi. Visitors get to the gallery through The Approach Tavern below, entering an elegant room whose high ceiling and large walls are capable of showing the largest paintings, sculptures and video works. Perhaps its main attraction to young artists has been that, while it has the look of a more upmarket gallery, it has until recently been run on a non-profit-making basis; bar takings were sufficiently high for rent for the space to be waived, sponsorship from breweries enabled commission from sales to be kept nominal. In the wake of recent sell-out shows, however, the gallery looks set to make the transition from alternative to a more commercially run venue.

How this will affect the programme remains to be seen. Director Jake Miller currently runs an eclectic mix of monthly shows championing unknowns, such as Phil Allen whose painted cardboard 'Skalextric' sculptures snaked around furniture and up the walls, as well as attracting a steady stream of fast-track young British stars including Peter Davies and Kerry Stewart. Peter Doig, the Tate's youngest artist-trustee, Matthew Higgs, whose *A–Z* featured more than 40 artists working with text, and painter Glenn Brown have been guest curators.

ADDRESS first floor, 47 Approach Road, London E2 9LY (0181–983 3878)
OPEN Thursday and Friday 13.00–18.00, Saturday and Sunday
12.00–18.00
TUBE Bethnal Green BUS D6, 8, 106, 253

The Showroom

The Showroom leases this single-storey building in Bonner Road, Bethnal Green from ACME, the artists' studio and housing association. Close to Interim Art and Chisenhale and neighbour to newcomers The Approach and Anthony Wilkinson Fine Art, it is an important, albeit unassuming part of the East End scene. Thanks largely to Kim Sweet, gallery director until summer 1998, The Showroom has earned a reputation for commitment to younger artists, commissioning new and often important works that have in a number of instances been pivotal to the advancement of early careers. Between four and six shows are held each year, emerging talent augmented by more established names. Though a revenue client of the London Arts Board, the gallery needs to secure additional support from public funds, trusts and through sponsorship for the realisation of each project and commission.

Not always the easiest space to fill, The Showroom has a wide frontage, tapering gradually to the rear, with a step between the two gallery spaces. The first space is well lit by a large picture window, and the rear gallery is roof-lit. In 1993 Francis Cape blocked off the gallery's long interior with a gloss-painted panelled wall. Viewers touched it, gingerly, to locate a hidden door leading to another space with wall and door and finally, in a wash of ivory sky lighting, the last and largest gloss wall. In 1996 Elizabeth Wright, an artist who is known for making ordinary objects out of scale, constructed a life-size replica of a corner of a 1950s bungalow in the front gallery. The second room of the gallery contained boxes filled with information about development proposals for the severely bombed East End – results of a 1943 questionnaire in which the majority of the local population expressed the desire to live in a 'small modern house' – and data showing that more than 96 per cent of new residential properties were instead built as flats. The

The Showroom

bungalow itself came to look like a distant, romantic dream.

Sam Taylor-Wood, who was nominated for the 1998 Turner Prize and included in the 1997 Venice Biennale, gained early recognition for her video installation 'Killing Time', commissioned by and shown at The Showroom in 1994. A multiple projection, it features four people filmed in four different settings waiting their turn to lip-synch a part in a German opera which unifies the separate images.

Recent exhibitions have included the first one-person UK shows of works by Simon Starling, who cast beer cans from an original found in Dessau, Germany, the one-time home to the Bauhaus, and Ceal Floyer, whose deceptively minimal pieces seem to have been shown almost everywhere – from the resolutely down-at-heel Cubitt Gallery to the forever upmarket Lisson.

Glaswegian artist and curator Kirsty Ogg recently filled the vacant director's post.

ADDRESS 44 Bonner Road, London E2 9JS (0181–983 4115)
OPEN Wednesday to Sunday 13.00–18.00
TUBE Bethnal Green BUS D6, 8, 106, 253

Anthony Wilkinson Fine Art

Anthony Wilkinson has had something of a peripatetic career. During the past five years he has done a stint as exhibitions organiser at The Eagle Gallery, curated shows at Cubitt Gallery, Henrietta House off Oxford Street, and in his former home in Great Ormond Street, giving early exposure to video-artist Jaki Irvine and painters Simon Callery and Chris Ofili along the way. In 1993 Callery made headlines when Charles Saatchi bought his entire show at the now-defunct Anderson O'Day gallery. Ofili, now represented by Victoria Miro (see page 5.2), has since moved into the A stream with solo museum shows at Southampton Art Gallery and the Serpentine Gallery and the 1998 Turner Prize.

Wilkinson's current space opened in May 1998 with biomorphic doodle paintings by Peter Ellis. A former greasy spoon flanked by sweat shop and kebab house in the decidedly unglamorous Cambridge Heath Road, it now boasts a cool concrete frontage and a series of light airy rooms on three floors. One of the first artists to sign up to the post-move Wilkinson stable was Angela de la Cruz, whose buckled, monochrome canvases were an instant hit in group shows at Laurent Delaye and Andrew Mummery galleries. In June 1998, at the same time as her first one-person show, Cruz made possibly one of the largest paintings ever. Measuring 14 by 10 metres, its broken frame was propped between the pillars of the Royal Festival Hall ballroom. Other gallery artists include Jessica Voorsanger, who in September 1998 invited more than a hundred art-world players to sign their names and have their hand prints cast in concrete in the style of Graumann's Chinese Theater in Hollywood.

ADDRESS 242 Cambridge Heath Road, London E2 9DA (0181–980 2662)
OPEN Thursday to Saturday 11.00–18.00, Sunday 12.00–18.00
TUBE Bethnal Green BUS D6, 26, 48, 55, 106, 253

east end

Interim Art

It looks like an unassuming Hackney terraced street, but Beck Road has played a key role in putting the East End on the artistic map. In the late 1970s, ACME, the artists' housing association now based in Bow, bought a number of these workers' cottages, selling them as live/work spaces to artists, including Helen Chadwick, who lived here until her death in 1996. Maureen Paley moved into her current property in 1979 and in 1984, when small domestic settings were unusual homes for contemporary art, began to show an ambitious line-up including Americans Jenny Holzer and Charles Ray. She has since become the doyenne of the do-it-yourself gallery with an international reputation. The size of Interim Art, two small downstairs rooms, belies Paley's ambition. She represents the 1997 Turner-Prize-winner Gillian Wearing and gave early exposure to nominee Angela Bulloch. The nearby Chisenhale Gallery has enabled gallery artists to realise larger projects such as Wearing's '10-16' video installation and Paul Noble's huge pencil drawings of his imaginary city, 'Nobson'.

Interim Art is a melting pot of cool young talent. Wolfgang Tillmans shows his photographs of fashion models and disaffected youth here and for his last solo exhibition hung a huge print of dappled woodland in the dingy railway arch that bisects the street. American 'bad-girl' Rita Ackermann chose Interim for her first solo show in this country. Recent exhibitions have had a bias towards young British artists, often straight out of college. Sarah Jones, who photographs bored middle-class adolescents, and David Rayson, who paints claustrophic suburban realist scenes, are just two of Paley's many protégés.

ADDRESS 21 Beck Road, E8 4RE (0171–254 9607)
OPEN Friday and Saturday 11.00–18.00
TUBE Bethnal Green BUS D6, 26, 48, 55, 106, 253

Flowers East

Angela Flowers Gallery opened in Soho in 1970, building its foundations on the sale of mostly English abstract painters including Terry Frost and Albert Irvine. In 1988 the gallery moved to Hackney, becoming Flowers East, which occupies two buildings on Richmond Road, one shared with Graham Paton Gallery (see page 1.34), the other adjacent to the art haulage firm Momart. Still identified with an older generation, it has been somewhat overlooked in recent years and has stuck quite successfully to a roster of gallery artists such as Peter Howson, whose somewhat melo-dramatic style suits perfectly his recent series of paintings based on *The Rake's Progress*, Nicola Hicks, whose skittish interpretations of animals hint at the darker side of human sexuality, and Bernard Cohen, known since the 1960s when he made brilliant, luminous spaghetti-like paint-ings, who continues to create dense, exquisitely crafted paintings combining figurative and abstract elements.

Recent surveys of painting and sculpture, *British Figurative Art*, proved that, despite the inclusion of Jenny Saville and Ron Mueck, the gallery is wide of the mark in terms of latest fashions. That said, in both shows there were impressive pieces – Andrew Stahl's painting of a huge half-eaten lolly and profile head, Tony Bevan's tense painting of a young man, hastily rendered in black and white, and disturbing polychromed wooden figures by Ana Maria Pachebo.

A separate graphics department publishes and sells limited-edition prints by a wide range of contemporary artists and in 1998 the gallery opened Flowers West in Santa Monica, California.

ADDRESS 199–205 Richmond Road, London E8 3NJ (0181-985 3333)
OPEN Tuesday to Sunday 10.00–18.00
TUBE Bethnal Green BUS D6, 48, 55, 106, 253

Paton Gallery

Graham Paton's first-floor gallery occupies the same not-terribly-attractive building as Flowers East (see page 1.32), close to the centre of Hackney. Not regarded as one of the major venues on the contemporary scene, it does, however, promote young artists, often fresh from the Royal College or Royal Academy Schools, who have had some recent success selling to collectors, both at home and abroad, including Charles Saatchi. If you're looking for the media-smart or for a quick fix then this is not the place to come, but somewhat slower, more traditional work, such as Kate Palmer's paintings of rusting architecture, is here in spades.

Rosie Snell, too, seems happy to idle in life's sidings. While stuck on a stationary train, she became fascinated by a line of disused goods wagons and later returned to investigate further. Her recent solo show featured paintings of rusting railway tracks and the similarly anonymous or overlooked – a lay-by and a perimeter fence – all loaded with late-twentieth-century melancholy. Her paintings of aircraft apparently abandoned in fields can be seen in the latest Saatchi Gallery publication, *The New Neurotic Realism*.

ADDRESS 282 Richmond Road, London E8 3QS (0181–986 3409)
OPEN Tuesday to Saturday 11.00–18.00, Sunday 12.00–18.00
TUBE Bethnal Green BUS D6, 48, 55, 106, 253

old street/shoreditch

Modern Art !nc   **2.2**
Morrison Judd   **2.4**
Lux Gallery   **2.6**
The Agency   **2.10**
30 Underwood Street   **2.14**

Modern Art !nc

The rise of Shoreditch has ensured two things: that rents are fast becoming prohibitively expensive, and that locals are forced to find somewhere quieter to drink, Soho perhaps, at the weekend. Undeterred, a number of galleries have opened in the area. Modern Art !nc is among the most recent, a rather swish well-designed space in Redchurch Street, off Shoreditch High Street and close to new kids on the block Morrison Judd (see page 2.4). Run by Stuart Shave, who has worked with Victoria Miro Gallery, it promises a substantial programme for 1999 including new work by Simon Bill, whose encaustic paintings on pegboard featuring mutant versions of teddy bears and the already hideous forms of Mr Blobby and Big Bird wander a thin line between humour, horror and reprehensible baseness.

For the inaugural show Tim Noble and Sue Webster, no strangers to the East-End scene, presented large glitzy Blackpool-style illuminated signs that alternate between brooding red and full-on disco assault, and a life-size version of the silhouette self-portrait bust seen in their 1997 solo show in nearby Rivington Street, also curated by Shave.

ADDRESS 73 Redchurch Street, London E2 7DJ (0171-729 2017)
OPEN Thursday to Sunday 11.00–18.00
TUBE Liverpool Street BUS 26, 35, 48, 55, 78, 242

Morrison Judd

Paul Morrison and Ben Judd are among the latest batch of Goldsmiths' graduates armed with perfect credentials and bags of confidence. Both have exhibited widely; Ben Judd's photographs of provocatively posed young women were recently seen at Deutsch Britische Freundschaft, Morrison's black and white cartoon-inspired landscape paintings were shown in 'Dumbpop' at the Jerwood Gallery in late 1998 and he has signed up to Asprey Jacques (see page 5.16). Judd has also written for *Flash Art* magazine, promoting the work of his peers, Morrison included.

Their gallery venture began in November 1998 with *Cluster Bomb*, a belt-and-braces affair featuring small works by more than 50 artists, from those still at college to the likes of Michael Craig-Martin, Bridget Riley, and Gerhard Richter, dotted around the rambling three-storey building off Shoreditch High Street. A clever and ambitious idea, but it failed to establish an immediate identity for the space. How the duo stamp their own personality remains to be seen. Solo shows of work by D J Simpson and John Chilver followed.

ADDRESS 1 and 3 French Place, London E1 6JB (0171–729 8402)
OPEN Friday and Saturday 12.00–18.00
TUBE Liverpool Street BUS 26, 35, 48, 55, 78, 242

Lux Gallery

London Electronic Arts has been a respected and significant part of the city's art scene for a number of years. As well as making its 30-year archive of artists' films and videos available to galleries and museums world-wide, it has commissioned projects by the likes of Gillian Wearing and Mark Wallinger, released compilations selected by writers and curators including Gregor Muir and Jonathan Watkins, and provided the latest facilities to artists working in increasingly high-tech media. Now merged with the London Filmmakers' Co-op, the LEA Gallery has changed its name to Lux.

The LEA Gallery – a first-floor space with views across Hoxton Square through large picture windows which are sometimes used for night-time projections – opened as part of the swish multimedia Lux Centre in autumn 1997. Initial commissions included Elizabeth Wright's 'Pizza delivery moped enlarged to 145% of its original size', which sits incongruously on the landing, and Darrell Viner's 'Light Curtain', rows of LEDs that are activated as you use the trendy steel-grid staircase. Angela Bulloch provided one of her seat-operated installations. From the LEA archives, she chose four videos that played constantly. As you sat on a bench facing one of the screens, sound was added to vision. Bulloch offered a weird and witty selection including the Duvet Brothers' video for New Order's 'Blue Monday' and Sadie Bening's slackerly romantic black-and-white short about rolling cigarettes and roller-skating around Coney Island.

Centrepiece of the first programme was Jane and Louise Wilson's terrific, frenetically edited film, 'Stasi City'. Shot in the abandoned Stasi headquarters in Berlin, it roams the deserted corridors, up and down the two-person paternosters, into interrogation rooms and offices. A slow-moving foray into an operating theatre adds to the sense of horror associated with the *Staatssicherheit*.

old street/shoreditch

Lux Gallery

At the time of opening I commented in *Time Out* that the project as a whole gave off conflicting signals. While most East End spaces struggle to survive, the LEA is unabashedly flash, reflecting the gentrification of the area. And, while the Wilson Twins represent the best of film and video work being produced today, the collective Housewatch, whose series of short ambient films were projected on to a mock-Victorian conservatory erected in Hoxton Square, displayed a tendency to elevate style over content.

ADDRESS Lux Centre, 2–4 Hoxton Square, London N1 6NU (0171–684 2785)
OPEN Wednesday to Friday 12.00–19.00, Saturday and Sunday 12.00–18.00
TUBE Old Street BUS 26, 48, 55, 67, 149, 242, 243 to Shoreditch Town Hall

The Agency

One of the few galleries remaining in the achingly fashionable and now utterly unaffordable Charlotte Road, since the early 1990s The Agency has maintained a programme of sporadic shows with a conceptual bias by mostly young British and European artists including Fergal Stapleton, a master of the uneventful who played with the gallery lighting, training a spotlight on to an electric flex trailing down the wall and annoying visitors with a persistently flickering bulb. In 1997 the gallery staged a miniretrospective of the work of Erlend Williamson, whose life was tragically ended the previous year in a climbing accident. Williamson made lowbudget, highly affecting and often hilarious work, taking the rather pious land art of artists such as Richard Long and Andy Goldsworthy and injecting it with a toxic urban feel.

'Insignificance', a show themed around the notion of the *femme fatale*, featured Rebecca Warren's collections of objects – a shell, a scrunchie, knickers filled with bits of carpet fluff, and a wasp trapped in a jam jar – perched precariously on grubby plinths and titled 'Every Aspect of Bitch Magic', poking fun at she-devil sorcery. Also included was a video montage using clips of *film-noir* sirens and a more recent crop of (anti) heroines by Bea de Souza, and Mary Beth Edelson's handprinted images on chiffon of stars such as Sigourney Weaver and Grace Jones.

Edelson, from the 1970s' wave of American feminists, was given a solo show in the summer of 1998. This included posters of Leonardo's 'The Last Supper' in which the heads of the disciples are replaced with photographs of women artists, and an ongoing piece, 'Story Gathering Box', which invited visitors to answer four questions printed on cards – 'What did your father teach you about men?'; What did your father teach you about women?'; 'What did your mother teach you about

The Agency

men?'; What did your mother teach you about women?' – with answers ranging from 'They're only good for sex' to 'We're the greatest'. The 1998 programme ended with work by Jane Hilton, Tim Noble, and Sue Webster.

ADDRESS 35–40 Charlotte Road, London EC2A 3QT (0171–613 2080)
OPEN Tuesday to Friday 11.00–18.00, Saturday 11.00–16.00
TUBE Old Street BUS 26, 48, 55, 243, 505

30 Underwood Street

The rather dank staircase leads to a large basement space that has become one of the more serious and long-standing alternative venues for cross-discipline work by young artists and, recently, more established players from the international scene, and art-historical shows, notably the first UK exhibition of Fluxus artist Tatsumi Orimoto. Young Brits to have shown here include Neil Miller, whose 1996 show featured sci-fi constructions executed with the skill of a ham-fisted back-bedroom enthusiast, and self-portrait photographs in which the artist spews up green slime, and Stephen Elson, who covered the floor with polyurethane tiles with diagonal ridges that made optical patterns, like an industrial-strength Bridget-Riley-inspired carpet. Matt Mitchell exploited the magic of ultraviolet light, using thin strips to suggest a full-scale swimming pool and diving board in the darkened space.

The 1998 programme was dominated by a major show of work by Hermann Nitsch. When he last showed in London in 1966 his performance at the ICA, part of Gustave Metzger's 'Destruction in Art Symposium' was broken up by police because it involved killing geese on stage. In 1957 Nitsch and Otto Muehl founded Vienna Actionism and later developed his own 'Orgies Mysteries Theatre' – ritualistic performances in which animals are regularly slaughtered and humans adopt the poses of sacrifice and martyrdom as a means of shaking people from, and drawing explicit attention to, the slumber of normality, which he has described as 'insipid vegetation'. Videos of these highly choreographed performances, shown at Underwood Street, show performers naked, blindfolded and paraded on stretchers or crucifixes while animal carcasses are bled on to or laid across their bodies. In August 1998, to wide media scrutiny, he staged a six-day blood-fest at his castle in Burgenland, northern Austria.

30 Underwood Street

The year ended with photographs and text pieces recording an eight-week journey made by Nick Waplington, who has previously photographed himself in some of the world's most polluted places and here, in images of empty streets and airport lounges, conveyed some of the dislocation felt by the traveller.

ADDRESS 30 Underwood Street, London
N1 7JX (0171–336 0884)
OPEN Friday to Sunday 13.00–18.00
TUBE Old Street BUS 55, 243, 505

clerkenwell

Laure Genillard Gallery **3.2**
Andrew Mummery Gallery **3.4**

Laure Genillard Gallery

Laure Genillard is one of the many gallerists to have made the journey east. This first-floor warehouse space on Clerkenwell Road is twice the size of Genillard's former premises in Foley Street but feels much bigger. A stable of young multimedia artists from the UK and Europe now benefits from an airy showroom with picture windows overlooking the street plus, to the rear, a smaller room ideal for showing film and video work. Padraig Timoney was first to profit from the move, complementing a sculpture consisting of a harshly lit blank video cassette mounted on a plinth with more atmospheric paintings. In June 1998 Swiss artist Sylvie Fleury continued her love/hate affair with the fashion industry. 'Life can get heavy, mascara shouldn't' included a tattoo-like wall painting of pink flames and the video 'Gucci Satellite', a kind of in-car road movie which focused only on the driver's stylish footwear.

Genillard painters are generally of the non-drip variety: Duo Alice Stepanek and Steven Maslin make highly contrived pictures of anonymous landscapes; Dan Hays, who had some success with his immaculate paintings of hamsters, hit the big time when he ditched them in favour of their empty cages. In 1997 he won the prestigious John Moores Prize, beating off stiff competition from the likes of Chris Ofili and Gary Hume. Recent group shows *Cloth-Bound*, which included Steven Gontarski, Alix Pearlstein and Marilyn Minter, and *Zooming on Patterns*, featuring Dan Hays and sickly-sweet abstracts by Daniel Sturgis, have focused on the themes of decoration, ornament and the resurgence of craft-based skills such as textile art and embroidery.

ADDRESS 82–84 Clerkenwell Road, London EC1M 5RJ (0171-490 8854)
OPEN Tuesday to Saturday 11.00–18.00
TUBE Farringdon BUS 55, 505

Andrew Mummery Gallery

This basement warehouse space, a former home of the Museum of Installation (see page 14.12), incorporates a gallery and project room from which Andrew Mummery runs a series of elegant understated exhibitions. An exploratory approach to painting characterises many of the artists he shows. Louise Hopkins takes as a starting point the fussy bourgeois patterns typified by a Laura Ashley print. Reversing the fabric, she reiterates the pattern in deathly pale shades and sepia tones. For her last one-person exhibition in October 1996 she also whited out the musical scores to various soppy love songs so that the surfaces hovered between being read as music and pure white-on-white abstraction *à la* Robert Ryman. The group show *Stepping Out* included Elizabeth Macgill's snapshots of aerobatics displays lovingly stitched on to canvas, and a series of monochrome canvases crumpled and broken and placed dejectedly in the corners of the gallery by Angela de la Cruz. A year later, *Stepping Up* provided an international companion piece with swirling abstracts by US-based painter David Reed, and a witty monochrome of drooping pink dots by French artist Bernard Frize.

The project room, to the rear of the gallery, continues Mummery's taste for the low-key; interventions by the likes of Stuart Taylor and Stefan Altenburger are generally slight, sometimes barely visible. Javier Marchan, however, painted the walls blush pink and provided inflatable sofas for viewers to watch his frenetically edited four-part video, 'No-Substance'.

ADDRESS 33 Great Sutton Street, London EC1V 0DX (0171–251 6265)
OPEN Tuesday to Saturday 11.00–18.00
TUBE Farringdon BUS 4, 43, 55, 505

warren street area

Robert Prime 4.2

Duncan Cargill Gallery 4.6

Greengrassi 4.8

Lotta Hammer 4.10

Robert Prime

A very English-sounding name for a gallery run by Italian directors Tommaso Corvi Mora and Gregorio Magnani. Situated in Warren Street, close to Duncan Cargill Gallery and Greengrassi and a short walk from Lotta Hammer Gallery, since opening in 1996 Robert Prime has shown work by both home-grown and international artists. The gallery represents 1997 Turner-Prize-nominee Angela Bulloch, whose bastardised modernist furniture is activated when sat upon, triggering a variety of sounds, and Liam Gillick, who, in his installation 'The What if? Scenario', filled the gallery with otherworldly *Star-Trek*-inspired inventions made from coloured plastics and brushed aluminium.

But perhaps the greatest contribution the gallery has made to the London scene has been its regular exhibitions of American and, in particular, European artists, introducing British audiences to names rarely seen in this country. French artist Dominique Gonzalez-Foerster took full advantage of a gallery space produced by knocking together existing rooms by creating three environments derived from a trip to India, each consisting of a handful of holiday snaps, a piece of furniture, a light and a wall painted in rich sunshine hues.

Since the late 1970s the German artist Candida Höfer has made photographs notable for their sense of detachment and stark composition. Her subjects are communal rooms in buildings across Europe; in September 1996, she filled the gallery with these blank and beautiful images of civic spaces.

In March 1997 Kai Althoff, also from Germany, showed an installation, a selection of watercolours, and an elongated gatefold sleeve for one of his records. Large sheets of acetate decorated with naïve flowers and seed-pod motifs hung from the ceiling. Beyond this makeshift glade lay a hut covered with wickerwork-effect paper in which illuminated

Robert Prime

papier-mâché heads with grimacing faces sat among empty wine bottles, pages torn from magazines and a flex with bare wires. The clues were unyielding, part innocent afternoon with paste and glue, part bizarre ritual.

American Jim Isermann reflects a West-Coast sensibility in his quilted and woven sculpture and wall-hangings. Camping up po-faced minimalism, for his first one-person show in this country he presented four cubes covered in plaid material and a series of hangings that ranged from subtle rhythmic greens to a clash of acid-hued daisy motifs.

ADDRESS 60–61 Warren Street,
London W1P 5PA (0171–916 6366)
OPEN Tuesday to Friday 11.00–18.00,
Saturday 14.00–18.00
TUBE Warren Street BUS 10, 24, 29, 73

Duncan Cargill Gallery

Duncan Cargill set up on his own in 1996, having worked for Karsten Schubert, and opened in Warren Street in September 1997. The space, a disused car showroom set into a Georgian terrace, is a throwback to the second-hand-car dealing that supported the area from the 1950s to the 1970s. Renovated by Theis and Khan Architects, it provides a large front space with an office and showing room under skylights at the rear. Completely glazing the 5-metre-wide shopfront got the architects shortlisted for the 1998 Camden Environmental Awards, and has the effect of blurring the distinction between street and gallery.

The space itself is versatile enough to cater for Cargill's programme, a mixed bag mainly by London-based artists. During December 1997, Sarah Staton conflated the polite pastimes of appliqué and stitching with bawdy humour. 'Spectacular Chunder Field' read the hanging in the window, painted with elegant stains and backed with vomit-inducing lime-green fabric; the proximity to such bastions of good taste as Heal's and Purves and Purves giving these defective drapes their edge. During summer 1998 Mark Cannon crammed in three different approaches to painting, ranging from old pieces of Formica cut into rectangles and assembled in the manner of hard-edge abstraction to reproductions of international symbols reproduced large on canvas.

The rather corporate monochrome paintings of Peter Davis and Mike Stubbs, photographs by Shizuka Yokomizo, who for her last solo exhibition turned her attention to friends sleeping, and matchstick models of former homes by Cath Pearson can also be found here.

ADDRESS 22 Warren Street, London W1P 5DD (0171-388 3603)
OPEN Tuesday to Friday 11.00–18.00, Saturday 11.00–15.00
TUBE Warren Street BUS 10, 24, 29, 73

Greengrassi

A relative newcomer to the London art scene, Cornelia Grassi has brought a wealth of international talent to her modest first-floor gallery in Fitzroy Street. Scouring Europe and her native America rather than relying on the kudos of young Brits, she has, like the neighbouring Robert Prime Gallery, given relatively obscure artists – Alessandro Pessoli, Frances Stark, for example – their first UK shows.

Better known to English audiences is Jennifer Bornstein, who featured in *Sightings* at the ICA in 1998. For her February 1998 solo show she photographed herself beside early-teen US kids, affecting their expressions and donning regulation T-shirts, baggy shorts and trainers but inevitably looking too grown-up, too self-conscious really to fit in. During summer 1998 the gallery showed prints by Lari Pittman, in tandem with his solo show at the ICA. His queeny, queasy images are an assault on the eyes. Sporting a rash of Ricki-Lake-style cat calls, patches of 1950s deco, credit-card motifs, assorted figures, foliage and genitalia, they revel in the identity crises of the late-twentieth-century metropolis. A perfect illustration of the uncontrollable toxic city, they are also perfectly mannered, better suited to print than to the large, somewhat inert paintings at the ICA.

During December 1998 Grassi gave the gallery over to three young artists: *The Origin of Parties* featured small abstract paintings by Tomma Abts, assemblages by recent Royal-College-graduate Steve Dowson, and a circle of laced-together trainers by Gareth Jones. The 1999 programme includes new work by Pae White and paintings of pneumatically enhanced housecoat-wearing female figures by Lisa Yuskavage.

ADDRESS 39c Fitzroy Street, London W1P 5HR (0171-387 8747)
OPEN Friday and Saturday 11.00–19.00
TUBE Warren Street BUS 10, 24, 29, 73

Lotta Hammer

Opening in March 1996, Lotta Hammer has been central to the rejuve-nation of the Foley Street area, to the north of Oxford Street, which, with the demise of Karsten Schubert Gallery and Laure Genillard's move to Clerkenwell, looked set to become something of a wasteland. With Robert Prime and Duncan Cargill Gallery in Warren Street, and Cornelia Grassi's showroom in Fitzroy Street, Fitzrovia is once again an enclave of thriving small commercial spaces.

Lotta Hammer has since settled in to a programme of British and inter-national newcomers, interspersed with more established names. During the gallery's first month a project space, 'Cleveland', run by critic and curator Andrew Renton, was started on adjacent gallery premises, with the aim of creating a dynamic between an alternative, or at least non-profit-making, space with a solely commercial enterprise. Between the two spaces, there was a total of 18 exhibitions in the first year. By 1997, however, the practical needs of the commercial venture meant that 'Cleve-land' was subsumed by Lotta Hammer, adding a further showing space to otherwise skinny premises.

Among the young British-based artists shown here are Mariele Neudecker, who makes models of Caspar-David-Friedrichesque land-scapes sealed in glass vitrines, Graham Gussin, whose deceptively simple objects and images prove time and space to be unstable referents, and sports fanatic Roderick Buchanan, who, in his photographs of football players in Glasgow wearing an assortment of strips, explored notions of fantasy, success and cultural identity.

Liz Arnold is one of the few painters to show here. Her carefully constructed cartoony paintings first came to prominence in the 1996 BT New Contemporaries exhibition which toured from Camden Arts Centre. For her last solo show, the mix of brightly coloured anarchic bugs

Lotta Hammer

warren street area

Lotta Hammer

in toxic industrial locations gave way to more sombre parkscapes and psychologically intense interiors, unpopulated or featuring a diminutive cat-woman wearing a 'Protect me from what I want' T-shirt, or reclining in a deck chair on a carpet of cigarette butts.

ADDRESS 51 Cleveland Street, London W1P 5PQ (0171–636 2221)
OPEN Monday to Friday 10.00–18.00, Saturday 10.00–17.00
TUBE Goodge Street BUS 10, 29, 73 to Goodge Street Underground

cork street area

Victoria Miro Gallery 5.2
Michael Hue-Williams 5.6
Waddington Galleries 5.8
Entwistle 5.12
Asprey Jacques 5.16
Stephen Friedman Gallery 5.20

Victoria Miro Gallery

Victoria Miro has maintained a high-quality programme throughout the 1990s, defying the recession when most galleries in the vicinity floundered. Her ground-floor gallery has often been the main reason for visiting the Cork Street area and even now, with neighbours such as Stephen Friedman and Entwistle, she is generally regarded as the major player.

Chris Ofili, Abigail Lane and *enfants terribles* Jake and Dinos Chapman are among the high-profile YBAS on Miro's books. Ofili, famous for his canvases of colliding swirls, lavish dots and lumps of elephant dung, rounded off 1998 by winning the Turner Prize. Lane proved there was more to her than bottom-print wallpaper, showing in January 1998 a nervously intense looped film of fluttering pigeons confined within a small space. The Chapmans, meanwhile, finally got round to completing their GCSE exams in art, displaying the results in a one-off show in their premises in Fashion Street, E1.

Miro also represents Peter Doig, who came to prominence in the early 1990s with a series of large-scale canvases remarkable for their intense atmosphere, accentuated colour and sumptuous detail. Figurative elements – such as a house, canoe or lone person – were seen through a dense web of marks and drips that, as well as signifying trees, reeds or snow, could be read as a separate and intricate painterly language. In 1995 Doig was shortlisted for the Turner Prize and won the prestigious John Moores Prize. A major solo exhibition was held at the Whitechapel Art Gallery in 1998 (see page 1.2).

As with most commercial London venues, there is a sense that Victoria Miro is looking beyond London for her next crop of young stars. Recent debuts include Thai artist Udomsak Krisanamis, who collages large areas of canvas with fragments of newsprint, painting out the type to leave only

the white ovals from the middle of the letter O, and Australian-born Tracey Moffatt, whose 1998 solo show of photographs set in the outback circled the racially and sexually charged narrative of a white woman giving birth to an Aboriginal child.

During January and february 1999, the gallery showed new paintings and drawings by American artist Robin Lowe, whose harshly lit portraits of defiant children featured in *Young Americans 2* at the Saatchi Gallery in 1998.

ADDRESS 21 Cork Street, London W1X 1HB
(0171-734 5082)
OPEN Monday to Friday 10.00–17.30,
Saturday 11.00–13.00
TUBE Green Park BUS 8, 9, 14, 19, 38

Michael Hue-Williams

One of Cork Street's less visible galleries, Michael Hue-Williams often surprises with the calibre of artists on show. While Victoria Miro Gallery occupies the prime spot downstairs, poetic work by the likes of James Turrell, Hiroshi Sugimoto and Tony Bevan can be found at this first-floor space. In January 1998, Bevan showed three large paintings, two of empty corridors, the third a mass of tangled lines that slowly reveals itself as a man's head.

In February and March 1998 the gallery showed Sugimoto's photographs of the Hall of Thirty Bays in Kyoto, a 90-metre-long Buddhist temple in which rows of near-identical life-sized statues of the Senju Kannon are housed; legend has it that among these statues worshippers will eventually find the face of their true love. Sugimoto's photographs, shot at just above eye level so that the figures' serried ranks fill each frame, eliminate any sense of scale and suggest an infinity of sacred beings on to which dreams and narratives can be projected. More examples of his beguiling photographs were seen at the Photographers' Gallery when he was shortlisted for the 1998 Citibank Private Bank Photography Prize.

During June 1998 the gallery showed an interesting early Turrell projection of two rectangles of coloured light, one blue, one red, which seemed to hover between phenomenological investigation and transcendent experience. Without the technical finesse of his later work, it seemed more grounded in reality and stronger for it. Huge woodcuts of woods and streams by Franz Gertsch were shown in October, followed by sculpture by Stephen Cox.

ADDRESS 21 Cork Street, London W1X 1HB (0171-434 1318)
OPEN Monday to Friday 9.30-17.30
TUBE Green Park BUS 8, 9, 14, 19, 38

Waddington Galleries

Leslie Waddington studied art history in Paris, then worked in the gallery of his father, Victor, before going it alone in 1966, and although Waddington Galleries may not be the all-powerful institution it once was, with spaces at numbers 11, 12 and 34 it still takes up a sizeable chunk of Cork Street. Showing a mix of modernist masters such as Dubuffet, Leger, Matisse, Miro and Max Ernst, often alongside British artists ranging from Ben Nicholson to Zebedee Jones, the programme could either be viewed as reflecting a desire to put British art into a broader context, to promote internationalism, or, as is often the case, a mish-mash of styles that makes little visual or historical sense. Either way a visit is worthwhile for the classic art that one would not ordinarily see in a commercial gallery.

Of the contemporary scene, the gallery deals mostly in painting both by elder statesmen and young stars. Michael Craig-Martin, Millard Professor at Goldsmiths' College since 1994, is generally regarded as the man behind the YBA phenomenon of the 1990s and, as a Tate artist-trustee, has a close association with developments at Bankside. An esteemed teacher whose influence spawned the confidence of the Damien-Hirst generation and beyond, his own work, last shown here in spring 1997, is a suitably sophisticated, conceptually based examination of the way we view or think we know objects and images in the world. Since the 1970s he has concentrated on a stock of about 200 standardised images of everyday objects, pictorial readymades which are then repro-duced as wall drawings in black and red tape, in which the objects are overlaid so that they assume an almost sculptural presence, or as paintings in which arrangements of objects – with differing scale and perspective – float on brightly coloured grounds.

Since 1990 the gallery has also represented Goldsmiths' protégés

Waddington Galleries

Fiona Rae and Ian Davenport, both of whom were shortlisted for the Turner Prize in 1991. Davenport, famous for his large canvases of repeated drips of household gloss paint, changed tack somewhat for his last solo show, confronting the viewer with a single form, an arch made by pouring on to a base colour a pool of gloss, licked by a third layer which stops short of initial form, to create a wavering line. Fiona Rae continues her full-scale assault on the visual languages of high modernism and popular culture, disguising her sampled riffs in ever more seamless, often stunning paintings.

Recent additions to the stable are Zebedee Jones, a casualty of Karsten Schubert's closure, whose heavily worked, almost wheezing mono-chromes first came to public consciousness in *Unbound: Possibilities in Painting* at the Hayward Gallery in 1994, and Michael Landy, whose 'Scrapheap Services' – a fictional, ironic yet pointedly political 'cleaning company' complete with mannequins of uniformed employees and a vast shredder for disposing of the hundreds of tiny figures Landy had cut out from beer cans and discarded packaging – was unsubtle but one of the most memorable exhibitions of 1996, when it appeared at Chisenhale.

ADDRESS 11, 12 and 34 Cork Street, London W1X 2LI (0171–437 8611)
OPEN Monday to Friday 10.00–17.30, Saturday 10.00–14.00
TUBE Green Park BUS 8, 9, 14, 19, 22, 38

Entwistle

One of several new galleries to inject life into the flagging Cork Street area, Entwistle works with young artists from the UK and imports an eclectic mixture from Europe and the US. Mark Sladen, director for contemporary art, cut his teeth writing for *Frieze* and *Art Monthly* magazines, and has successfully tapped into current trends, particularly the rise of figurative painting among second-wave YBAs. Among the emerging talent represented are painters Nicky Hoberman and Jason Brooks, both of whom were included in *The New Neurotic Realism*, a survey of Charles Saatchi's latest purchases. Brooks paints portraits of friends and colleagues in the style of the great American hyper-realist Chuck Close. Hobermann's slightly blurred images of young girls, either singly or in groups, are cropped severely against brightly coloured backgrounds, tempering wistful nostalgia with a tougher aesthetic.

Reflecting the current zeal for images of childhood, Entwistle also shows Los-Angeles-based artist Amy Adler, whose exhibition comprising photographs of male adolescents engaged in stereotypically boyish activities – shooting marbles, playing with a train set – was titled 'The Problem Child', after a study by the Austrian psychiatrist Alfred Adler.

Less modish and more interesting are Charles Avery, Siobhan Hapaska, and Sue Arrowsmith. Arrowsmith, who rules black lines on to surfaces of mostly white gesso, studied textiles at Goldsmiths'; her clean-cut paintings blend a nostalgia for grand American abstraction with the impeccable styling of a bespoke suit. For his last solo show, *Portraits of People Who Never Existed*, Avery presented a cycle of portraits spanning the entire history of an imaginary civilisation. Hapaska, who was included in the 1997 *Documenta* exhibition in Kassel, Germany, makes opalescent sculptures that seem to be on the point of morphing into recognisable forms and hyper-real wax figures. For her 1995 show at the ICA, she

included 'Here', a futuristic bed complete with sheepskin cover, upon which viewers could recline, connect themselves to an oxygen supply and drift off to sleep. Her last solo exhibition at Entwistle included a rather wonderful motorised tumbleweed and a typically slinky sculpture trapped in heavy wooden stocks.

ADDRESS 6 Cork Street, London W1X 2EE (0171–734 6440)
OPEN Monday to Friday 10.00–18.00, Saturday 11.00–16.30
TUBE Green Park BUS 8, 9, 14, 19, 38

Asprey Jacques

Charles Asprey – who as founder-director of Ridinghouse Editions commissioned projects and editions from YBA stars such as Jake and Dinos Chapman and Sam Taylor-Wood – and Alison Jacques – who has worked as curator of the Contemporary Art Programme at the British School in Rome and more recently at Waddington Galleries – are a young team set to make waves in the traditional stronghold around Cork Street. Their new gallery provides 150 square metres of exhibition space over three floors of an eighteenth-century building in Clifford Street for a mix of predominantly young international artists. Asprey has commented that 'In the current post-*Sensation* YBA climate, it is essential that we broaden our horizons and look outside London to new centres of contemporary art such as Berlin' and, true to his word, Asprey Jacques' inaugural exhibition was by young Germans Manfred Pernice, who added low-tech constructions to the immaculate space, and Daniel Pflumm, whose video consisted of corporate logos flashed at dizzying speed before the eyes of viewers.

Asprey Jacques are also the first commercial space in the UK to offer a residency programme for an artist to live and work in London. First to benefit was Jaspar Joseph-Lester, whose recent work has involved the reconstruction of optical instruments such as overhead projectors in order to display their inner workings. In 1999 residencies include Swedish artist Roger Andersson.

British artists to sign to the gallery include Jane Simpson, who was included in *Sensation* at the Royal Academy in 1997 and created 'Folly', a beautifully suggestive metal form covered in a layer of ice for her solo exhibition at The Approach through September and October 1998. In December 1998 the gallery presented landscape-inspired sculpture by Tania Kovats and Barbara Hepworth, the first in a series of exhibitions

Asprey Jacques

in which work by a young artist is shown alongside that of a contemporary or modern master. Kovats' sculptures are derived from real land forms as well as from picture postcards and images in *National Geographic*. The small, rather beautiful structures appear to be embedded in or eroded from immaculate white plinths; viewed from one angle they confer a minimalist aesthetic, from another they lay bare a romantic intent. The comparison with Hepworth hinges on belief. Hepworth famously said 'I, the sculptor, *am* the landscape' and her three sculptures from the 1970s, shortly before her death, convey her lifelong conviction perfectly.

Asprey Jacques also plans a number of off-site projects and one-off collaborations, the first of which was a film shot in late 1998 in Rome by Cerith Wyn Evans.

ADDRESS 4 Clifford Street, London W1X 1RB
(0171–287 7675)
OPEN Tuesday to Friday 10.00–18.00,
Saturday 11.00–17.00
TUBE Green Park BUS 8, 9, 19, 22, 38

Stephen Friedman Gallery

In summer 1995, excited by the work being produced by young British artists, American Stephen Friedman opened this shop-fronted showroom in Old Burlington Street. He had previously worked as a private dealer and as a specialist at Christie's. The Gregory-Phillips-designed gallery comprises an exhibition space at the front, with a smaller viewing room and office at the rear leading to an external courtyard where outdoor works are occasionally shown. For the gallery's inaugural exhibition Anya Gallaccio hung the front room with an extended daisy chain of red gerberas that gradually dried and faded to brown. In the viewing room she placed a glass-topped table covered with burning white candles.

Friedman's love of British art has been borne out by a stable of young British-born stars. Kerry Stewart's unnerving sculptures include the Scooby-Doo-style 'Ghost' and an enlarged superhero cloak. Yinka Shonibare troubles readings of ethnicity and appropriation by using mass-produced 'African' fabric in a variety of guises: as painting support, or to reinterpret sumptuous Victorian dresses, for example. The fabric is in fact designed in Indonesia and produced in factories in the north of England for export to Africa. Newcomer David Thorpe, who makes intricate paper collages that depict a glamorous 'cocktail hour' city, was included in the Martin Maloney-curated *Die Young Stay Pretty* exhibition at the ICA in November 1998.

Friedman also represents more established names from the international circuit including German sculptor Stephan Balkenhol, who reclaims the art of woodcarving to create ambivalent, inscrutable, rather melancholy figures, and Laotian-born sculptor Vong Phaophanit, whose 'Neon Rice Field', strips of neon placed beneath the surface of furrows of translucent rice, earned him a Turner-Prize nomination in 1993.

South African William Kentridge's star is in the ascendant. Included in 1997's *Documenta X* exhibition in Kassel, his nervy animated films, drawn in smudged charcoal, refer to his country's damaged history.

Through July 1998 the American pop-culture junkie Richard Phillips showed his large photo-realist portraits rooted in the girlie mags of the 1970s.

ADDRESS 25–28 Old Burlington Street, London W1X 1LB
(0171-494 1434)
OPEN Tuesday to Friday 10.00–18.00, Saturday 11.00–17.00
TUBE Green Park BUS 8, 9, 14, 19, 38

cork street area

dering street

Anthony d'Offay Gallery   **6.2**
Anthony Reynolds Gallery   **6.6**
Annely Juda Fine Art   **6.10**

Anthony d'Offay Gallery

With large ground- and first-floor spaces and a smaller building suitable for showing prints and works on paper, the Anthony d'Offay Gallery dominates Dering Street. The gallery deals in the most important international figures, dead and alive, and to its eternal credit still has a touch of glamour. The list of d'Offay artists is itself a roll-call of the major league: from masters such as Joseph Beuys, Andy Warhol, Willem de Kooning to Gilbert and George, Jeff Koons and Sigmar Polke, to Rachel Whiteread who, with some acrimony, left Karsten Schubert Gallery for d'Offay in 1996. Recent shows have included more than 60 new paintings by Gerhard Richter, a fantastic mini-retrospective of strategic word-and-image combiner Ed Ruscha, and a haunting installation by Christian Boltanski, who filled the lower gallery with metal cots reminiscent of operating tables, mortuary slabs or places of torture. Such is the calibre of gallery stock that even summer shows, usually a trawl through the vaults, are capable of unearthing new pieces by the likes of Anselm Kiefer and Louise Bourgeois.

Though it might seem that Anthony d'Offay has always had a keen nose for the cutting edge, he began in the late 1960s with shows of Vorticist art, and the then all-but-forgotten members of the Bloomsbury Set and Camden Town School. His foray into more avant-garde territory came during the 1970s, influenced by his wife Anne, then assistant keeper at the Tate.

More recently, Margot Heller, formerly director of Southampton City Art Gallery, has injected new blood into the stable, taking chances and raising eyebrows along the way. Among the latest additions are Martin Maloney, whose *faux-naif* paintings of still-lifes and lounging figures are perpetual opinion dividers. Others to enter the major-league have been Edward Smith and Stephanie Stewart – whose performance video works

Anthony d'Offay Gallery

recall the symbiotic and often fraught performances of 1970s team Ulay and Abramovic – and Richard Patterson, who is best known for his slick 'Motocrosser' series of paintings of a scaled-up toy and who for his last show conflated such unlikely bed fellows as the Spice Girls and Thomson the cat of telephone-directory fame.

More interesting to a British audience is the wealth of European and, particularly, young US artists that the gallery is capable of attracting. Belgian Johan Grimonprez' grim but gripping film of the history of skyjacking and US artist Ellen Gallagher's Agnes-Martinesque-style minimalism, which turns out to be composed of the exaggerated eyes and mouths of nineteent- century American minstrels, are highlights of an increasingly risky programme.

ADDRESS Dering Street, London W1R 9AA (0171–499 4100)
OPEN Monday to Friday 10.00–17.30, Saturday 10.00–13.00
TUBE Oxford Circus BUS 3, 7, 8, 12, 25, 53, 55, 73, 88, 139, 189

Anthony Reynolds Gallery

A small ground-floor gallery and a rather confusing basement space which is sometimes also used for showing. Dwarfed by the neighbouring Anthony d'Offay Gallery (see page 6.2), since the early 1980s the Anthony Reynolds Gallery has nonetheless attracted a roster of important international artists including Gerhard Merz, Nancy Spero, and Susana Solano, and represented some of the more conspicuous names among the YBA pack.

For *God*, his most recent solo exhibition, Mark Wallinger broke away from his obsession with class, money and status and showed 'Angel', a video shot at the foot of the escalators at Angel underground station. With dark glasses and a cane, Wallinger appears as an alarming, slightly crazed figure pacing the bottom step of the escalator while repeating the opening verse of 'The Gospel According to St John': 'In the beginning was the word and the word was God ...'. His speech seems slurred and in fact the film is being played backwards. The escalator is really moving downwards and the awkwardness of Wallinger's voice comes from reading the words in reverse. The sequence ends with him gliding upwards, bathed in light, to the climactic chorus of Handel's *Zadok the Priest*.

Georgina Starr – the darling of the international circuit for a couple of years – constructs elaborate, often frenzied scenarios that conflate fact and fantasy, frequently using incidents in her own life to trigger compellingly eccentric films and installations. Her 1994 installation at the gallery, 'Getting to Know You', recorded her attempts to find out about a man she had never met, a Dutch writer called Gerard Stigter, via a sample of his handwriting, his hand print, the hour of his birth, etc. In 1996, at the Tate Gallery's Art Now room (see page 12.14), she presented 'Hypnodreamdruff', a collection of sets, props and TV monitors in which viewers could visit an imaginary night-club called 'The Hungry Brain' and

Anthony Reynolds Gallery

observe its bizarre clientele, drop in on Starr's teenage bedroom and see a film of her acting out the female roles in *Grease*, or climb into the small caravan home of the mysterious Lionel-Ritchie-loving Dave.

Recent exhibitions prove Reynolds to have a shrewd sense of the latest trends. During September and October 1998 recent Goldsmiths' graduate Keith Farquhar showed paintings resembling science-textbook covers that are among the most human and beautiful pictures being made today.

ADDRESS 5 Dering Street, London W1R 9AB (0171–491 0621)
OPEN Monday to Saturday 10.00–18.00
TUBE Oxford Circus BUS 3, 7, 8, 10, 12, 25, 53, 55, 73, 88, 139, 189

Annely Juda Fine Art

This top-floor daylit space designed by the late Max Gordon has a hushed, almost reverential atmosphere. Founded in 1968 with the intention of bringing to wider attention the work of Russian avant-garde and constructivist artists Naum Gabo and Alexander Rodchenko, the gallery has gained a reputation for museum-standard exhibitions such as *The Non-Objective World 1914–18*. Rigorously researched summer shows such as 1998's *The Thirties*, which focused on a small group of artists including Piet Mondrian and Ben Nicholson who briefly lived near each other in Hampstead, are still leagues ahead of the sorry displays of gallery stock that fill most spaces during the quiet summer months.

Gallery artists tend towards old-school international heavyweights. Annely Juda first exhibited Christo in 1971 and in 1995, to coincide with his much publicised wrapping of the Reichstag building in Berlin, held its ninth Christo exhibition. In 1997, to a decidedly lukewarm critical response, David Hockney showed his latest series of sun-baked portraits and still-lifes.

But the gallery also represents a quieter, more poetic breed of British artist including painter Edwina Leapman, and Roger Ackling, who needs nothing more than a piece of found wood and a magnifying glass to create his magical scorched wall pieces.

Adding to this mix, the gallery regularly shows artists from the Far East, including Yuko Shiraishi, whose highly seductive minimalist paintings edge closer to site-specific territory, and Katsura Funakoshi, whose meditative wooden figures are carved from fragrant camphor wood. In 1997, while the Serpentine Gallery was undergoing refurbishment, Tadashi Kawamata used the discarded glazed gallery doors to create a stunning installation which rose through the floor from the showroom

Annely Juda Fine Art

below, and crept across the ceiling of Annely Juda's pristine gallery space.

The 1998 programme ended with work by Hamish Fulton, who for the past 30 years has charted his journeys through various landscapes, using photography and text to find an equivalent to the experience.

ADDRESS 23 Dering Street, London W1R 9AA (0171–629 7578)
OPEN Monday to Friday 10.00–18.00, Saturday 10.00–13.00
TUBE Oxford Circus BUS 3, 7, 8, 10, 12, 25, 53, 55, 73, 88, 139, 189

frith street/covent garden

Frith Street Gallery **7.2**
London Projects **7.6**
The Photographers' Gallery **7.10**

Frith Street Gallery

A beautiful series of modern and period rooms occupying two adjacent buildings, one seventeenth- and one nineteenth-century, in the heart of Soho. A former owner of number 60 was Nathaniel Home, a contemporary of Sir Joshua Reynolds. Horne's painting depicting Reynolds frolicking with a prostitute was expelled from a salon show at the Royal Academy. As a consequence Home opened number 60 as a private gallery, quite possibly the first-known private gallery in England.

Today it retains an air of quiet exclusivity. Jane Hamlyn founded the gallery in 1989 with the aim of showing works on paper. The 1994 expansion to incorporate the building next door created three extra gallery spaces capable of showing larger works by a strong list of gallery artists including 1998 Natwest-Painting-Prize-winner Callum Innes, 1998 Turner-Prize-nominee Tacita Dean, 1997-nominee Cornelia Parker, and Jaki Irvine, whose oblique series of films, 'Another Difficult Sunset', represented Ireland at the 1997 Venice *Biennale*. Perhaps the best of an increasingly authoritative stable is French painter Bernard Frize, whose ravishing abstracts are witty ripostes to much of the dry process-driven painting of recent years.

Photography, video and film have, in more recent years, become the gallery's forte; in April 1998 Craigie Horsfield's psychologically intense photographs were shown concurrently with Alexander Sokurov's five-and-a-half-hour film chronicling the lives of young Russian soldiers drafted to guard the border between Tadjikistan and Afghanistan. But drawing in particular looks fantastic in the space, as witnessed in *From Figure to Object*, a survey of sculptors' drawings presented in 1997 in collaboration with the now-defunct Karsten Schubert Gallery.

Pencil lead is also the preferred medium of gallery artist Fiona Banner, whose wall-sized hand-written texts describe films such as *Top Gun* from

a viewer's perspective and whose book *The Nam*, a 500-page tome which combines descriptions of several Vietnam films, was published by the gallery in 1997.

In January 1999, Belgian film-maker Chantal Ackerman showed extracts from 'D'Est', a film made on a journey through Germany to Moscow in 1992, and 'Jeanne Dielman, 23 Quai du Commerce, 1080 Bruxelles' of 1975 – the celebrated film of a middle-class housewife's domestic routine.

ADDRESS 59–60 Frith Street, London W1V 5TA (0171-494 1550)
OPEN Tuesday to Friday 10.00–18.00, Saturday 11.00–16.00
TUBE Tottenham Court Road BUS 8, 10, 19, 24, 25, 38, 55, 73, 176

frith street/covent garden

London Projects

London Projects was established in 1994, originally under the name of Marc Jancou Gallery which occupied the same building as Karsten Schubert Gallery in Foley Street, W1. Its current premises are in Frith Street, about a hundred metres from Frith Street Gallery towards Old Compton Street. Two first-floor rooms offers visitors the chance of seeing work by international artists including Polish-born Miroslaw Balka, who for his 1998 exhibition entitled *Out* continued his concern with the body, human presence, the idea of passage, memory and death, injecting a minimalist vocabulary of metal forms with a distinctly poetic sensibility. Gallery artists are a eclectic bunch, ranging from John Coplans, who photographs his ageing body, to Alexis Rockman, whose display cases filled with a mixture of stuffed animals, plastic models and plants ridicule attempts to control nature, either by classification or containment.

For his last solo exhibition, Charles Long, who featured in the first of the Saatchi Gallery's *Young Americans* exhibitions, toned down the garish colour schemes of his trademark half-sci-fi set/half-furniture biomorphs, lending a wittily co-ordinated *Elle Deco* feel. During the summer of 1998 Long was featured in *Preview*, a group show of artists scheduled for one-person exhibitions during the 1998–99 season. This also included Miguel Rio Branco, who has been exhibiting painting, photography and films in South America since 1964, and Michelle Fierro, whose canvases consist of little dabs, dollops and smudges of paint, sometimes squeezed straight from the tube and at other times scraped off the floor of a friend's studio. Scraps of paper and tiny fragments of fabric likewise interrupt the large areas of canvas the artist has left raw or hastily covered with uneven coats of acrylic paint.

London Projects also offers the chance to see established names rarely shown in this country. These included in December 1996 documentation

of seminal performances from 1971–73 by Chris Burden, most famous for being shot on stage by an assistant who was supposed only to graze him. In 1997, as a tribute to German artist Martin Kippenberger who died that year, the gallery showed 30 of the artist's drawings on headed hotel notepaper. Edgy, witty, sometimes chaotic, they highlighted the need for a full retrospective of this fascinating and multifaceted artist.

ADDRESS 47 Frith Street, London W1V 5TE (0171–734 1723)
OPEN Friday and Saturday 10.00–18.00
TUBE Tottenham Court Road BUS 8, 10, 19, 24, 25, 38, 55, 73, 176

The Photographers' Gallery

Britain's first independent gallery devoted to photography was founded in 1971 in a converted Lyons teashop at No. 8 Great Newport Street. The building now houses the Photographers' Gallery's main exhibition space and a bookshop. In 1980 the gallery also moved into No. 5 Great Newport Street, renamed Halina House after a generous benefactor. The first gallery in the country to show major names in world photography such as Kertesz and Lartigue, it has been instrumental in encouraging other leading galleries and museums to include photography in their programmes.

From *De Dam 7 Mei* (1997) which portrayed the tragic events in Dam Square, Amsterdam when dozens of people were killed and wounded by German soldiers, to Rineke Dijkstra's photographs of adolescents the world over, the recent programme has shown photography both in its earliest or documentary form and in its current guises as interchangeable with and reflecting the changing face of contemporary art. *Speed*, held in association with the Whitechapel Gallery during September 1998 (see page 1.2), included Doug Aitken's 'American International', a video installation that documents Ron Fringer's attempt to ride a supercharged motorbike down a racetrack at 190 mph, and Rachel Lowe's projection 'A Letter to an Unknown Person', in which the artist traces the view with marker pen on to the window of a fast-moving car.

Paul Wombell, who was appointed director in 1994, is keen to embrace the immense technological and artistic changes the medium is undergoing as it enters the twenty-first century – essential if the gallery is to remain valid. The 1999 programme includes *Mayday in the Global Nursery*, which explores the relationship between community and communication and evolves over time, with different displays continually changing at different rates.

The Photographers' Gallery

The gallery also hosts the annual Citibank Private Bank Photography Prize, now in its third year. Previous winners of the prestigious prize are Richard Billingham and, from a particularly strong shortlist in 1998, Andreas Gursky.

The print sales room offers one of the country's finest selections of original photographs and there is also a café.

ADDRESS 5 and 8 Great Newport Street, London WC2H 7HY (0171–831 1772)
OPEN Monday to Saturday 11.00–18.00, Sunday 12.00–18.00
TUBE Leicester Square BUS 24, 29, 176

the rest of w1

Laurent Delaye Gallery   **8.2**
Timothy Taylor Gallery   **8.6**
Sadie Coles HQ   **8.8**

Laurent Delaye Gallery

In the heart of London's busiest shopping area, this slightly dishevelled building provides three floors of light and airy showing space for a blend of British and international artists. The gallery opened in spring 1996 with sculptures by American artist and film-maker Beth B, followed by video installations by recent Goldsmiths' graduate Sacha Dieu. Early exhibitions – *Dissolution*, including Tracey Emin, Mark Wallinger and Gavin Turk, and *Dissolution: Made in the USA*, which brought to British attention the less-known Steve Di Benedetto, Cheryl Donegan and Nicole Eisenman – were lively and ambitious showcases for shifting attitudes towards painting on both sides of the Atlantic.

Driving Towards Distraction in June 1998 featured short films by Mark Dean, Milo Garcia, and Frederic Beaumes, who collaged fragments of home movies to the soundtrack to *Star Wars*. *Still* was a pointedly laconic summer show that pitted Marcus Taylor's series of bent and buckled 'Reflected Refrigeration Distortion' sculptures against the gloopy sagging gloss paintings of Alexis Harding, and James Casebere's 'Two Bunk Cell', a photograph of a tiny mock-up of a spartan interior.

Gallery artists are headed by a cast of increasingly prominent painters. Machiko Edmondson's cropped photorealist portraits display both technical virtuosity and a certain fanaticism for top models, pooches and even indie glum-rocker Nick Cave. During June and July 1998, Simon English, who was included in *Young British Artists III* at the Saatchi Gallery in 1994, showed new paintings featuring writhing bodies and bemused on-lookers. James Rielly, 1995 artist in residence at the Tate Gallery, Liverpool, has exhibited widely in Europe and was included in *Sensation* held at the Royal Academy in 1997. His second solo show, in October 1998, continued to probe themes of lost innocence and bodily or psychological violence. Rielly's stance is equivocal: he paints portraits of victims but,

Laurent Delaye Gallery

adding an extra pair of eyes, for example, he not only suggests fractured identity but makes the subject impossible to look at. They provoke knee-jerk reactions nonetheless. In 'Art and Immorality' published in *The Modern Review*, Julie Burchill argued that Rielly's paintings ought to be banned as they are a free licence to the 1990s' 'help-yourself paedophilia'.

ADDRESS 22 Barrett Street, St Christopher's Place, London W1M 5HP (0171-629 5905)
OPEN Tuesday to Friday 10.00–18.00, Saturday 12.00–18.00
TUBE Bond Street BUS 7, 8, 10, 12, 73, 88, 139, 189

the rest of w1

Timothy Taylor Gallery

Timothy Taylor's small rather charming gallery is tucked away in Bruton Place behind the designer stores of Bond Street. Since December 1996 he has specialised in representing established names, mostly abstract painters, with a bias towards Spain and the US. Not really cutting-edge, the gallery does, however, show important work neglected by the current vogue for all things young and British; the studied doodles and mannered abstract-expressionist riffs of Jonathan Lasker and the increasingly soft-focus grids and bars of Sean Scully, to name but two. Juan Uslé's highly choreographed arrangements of bravura brush marks, lattices and ribbons of paint were a highlight of the 1997–98 programme. In 1997 Julian Schnabel, who in many ways embodies the idea of 1980s' excess, showed new photographs, a bronze and a refreshingly animated painting.

The 1998 season included new work by Miquel Barcelo, who had not shown in this country since his Whitechapel exhibition in 1994. Barcelo creates a restless topography of paint, often studded with collage. Famous for throwing at the canvas almost anything, including food, he creates an impasto that wavers between a genuine expression of mood or locale and a deliberately weathered or aged 'look' that implies *gravitas*. At Timothy Taylor he presented subdued paintings with a more rigorous sense of structure to counteract the rather heroic theme of the artist in the landscape. Through summer and autumn the gallery showed three Latin-American artists – Julio Galan, Jose Bedia, and Ray Smith – in succession, followed by new paintings by Craigie Aitchison, in association with Waddington Galleries.

ADDRESS 1 Bruton Place, London W1X 7AD (0171-409 3344)
OPEN Monday to Friday 10.00–18.00, Saturday 11.00–14.00
TUBE Bond Street BUS 7, 8, 10, 12, 73, 88, 139, 189

Sadie Coles HQ

Sadie Coles opened this first-floor New-York-loft-style space in spring 1997 and immediately became the name to watch. A former director at the Anthony d'Offay Gallery, she has her eyes trained on the hippest of both the American and British scenes, plucking the relatively unknown and luring the established. First up were John Currin's paintings of blonde babes and matriarchs with impossible busts and cruelly palette-knifed faces. Next came Sarah Lucas, whose *The Law* was spread between HQ and a pre-gentrified warehouse space in St John's Street, Clerkenwell. In this dilapidated space, Lucas found the perfect home for her bawdy and ballsy work, which included a gyrating Ford Capri and a cardboard coffin.

Coles has since proved her commitment to off-site projects. She co-hosted works by David Falconer, whose mountain of rat casts announced the arrival of the Chapman Fine Arts in Fashion Street off Brick Lane, E1, plans further projects with the Chapmans, and, in October 1998, arranged a cinema presentation of Angus Fairhurst's animations. HQ also curates the art collection for trendy eateries The Atlantic Bar & Grill, Coast, and Mash, where drinkers are met by one of Don Brown's self-portrait sculptures and sit surrounded by a photo-mural of 1970s lifestyle ads cruelly doctored by John Currin.

Currin was one of the stars of *Young Americans 2* held at the Saatchi Gallery which also included HQ artists Laura Owens, who makes slow-revealing sceptical paintings of West-Coast landscapes and art-smart interiors, and Elizabeth Peyton, who makes star-struck portraits of latter-day demi-gods.

Coles was also the first to give 'bad girl' Sue Williams a solo UK show, by which time her paintings had progressed from explicit depictions of violence towards women to a more suggestive and sexy abstraction.

Sadie Coles HQ

Rising British stars include Simon Periton, maker of elaborate, often macabre doilies, and Daniel Oates who creates toys for mass production and surreal one-off Disneyesque sculptures.

In January 1999 Andren Zittel showed her 'Personal Panels', coloured rectangles of cloth that resemble abstract paintings and which can be worn as simple clothing.

ADDRESS 35 Heddon Street, London W1R 7LL (0171-434 2227)
OPEN Tuesday to Saturday 10.00–18.00
TUBE Piccadilly Circus BUS 3, 6, 12, 13, 15, 53, 88, 94, 109, 139, 159

north london

Saatchi Gallery   **9.2**
Camden Arts Centre   **9.8**

Saatchi Gallery

Britain's largest and most beautiful gallery looks like nothing from the street but behind the anonymous entrance lies 3000 square metres of former warehousing, converted magnificently in 1985 by Max Gordon. The spaces are designed perfectly for maximum effect, from the dimly lit foyer to the always thrilling step down into the huge expanse of whiteness. Though the gallery has given us exhibitions of such major international figures as Sol LeWitt, Andy Warhol and Bruce Nauman, it is, of course, for its exhibitions of young British art that it and its enigmatic owner are best known. Since spring 1992 there have been seven shows of work by YBAs including the most memorable sculptures of the decade – 'The Impossibility of Death in the Mind of the Living', Damien Hirst's shark, and 'Ghost', Rachel Whiteread's plaster cast of a living room. Add Gary Hume, Fiona Rae, Mark Wallinger, Jake and Dinos Chapman, Sarah Lucas, Gavin Turk and Chris Ofili to the list and Charles Saatchi's commitment to the scene becomes utterly apparent.

But what of the legendary man? Megalomaniac, saviour of contemporary art, committed collector, or dealer with dubious taste and too much cash? Charles Saatchi is famous for never giving interviews, adding mystique to his reputation. He doesn't attend his own private views but personally oversees the hanging of each show, tinkering with the installation up to the last minute. The man who made his career in advertising and whose most famous campaigns are the Silk Cut slash and the 1979 'Labour isn't Working' Tory-party election campaign is himself a doyen of the one-liner, borne out by his taste for the quick-fix in-your-face artwork with which British art of the last decade is synonymous.

To a large extent Saatchi *is* the contemporary-art market, and a shadow that seems to lurk in every studio and now every art college certainly in the capital, probably in the country. For young artists, having work

bought by Saatchi can mean the difference between affording a studio and continuing, or the dole. But the rather petrified *New Contemporaries* shows of recent years have revealed graduates making what they think he'll buy based on what he's just bought. The December 1998 sale of work from his collection – an off-loading of work by stars such as Damien Hirst and Rachel Whiteread – was held in order to raise money for bursaries at the main London colleges. Supreme benevolence or further proof of his stranglehold over successive generations?

There are those who argue that Saatchi buys too much. He certainly bulk buys, from exhibitions or directly from studios or degree shows, and often for knock-down prices. And when he sells on the effects can be devastating. Sandro Chia complained bitterly when, after collecting dozens of the Italian's figurative paintings in the 1980s, Saatchi sold them *en masse*.

Too much hinges on Saatchi, his obsessions and whims because of the dearth of collectors in this country. But regardless of how you regard him, his version of art history over the past decade has been far more exciting than anything anyone else has offered, and he has been crucial in generating the interest in young artists that still exists – a decade after *Freeze*, seven years after Hirst's now-withered shark, and two years after *Sensation* caused a rumpus at the Royal Academy.

So, what now? Saatchi is equated with young and British but over the past two years there have been solo shows of Americans Duane Hanson and Alex Katz, instalments of *Young Americans*, including the best of the much-touted LA scene, and *Young Germans,* with its not-so-young masters Thomas Schütte and Andreas Gursky. *Sensation* did bring about something of a hiatus, leaving vacant slots for new Damiens and Rachels. But the artists featured in the latest Saatchi publication, *The New*

Neurotic Realism, are by no means adequate successors to the throne. The title is itself a catch-all for the disparate and largely second-rate, an after-dinner witticism that sounds good, means nothing and should never have made it to the printers.

The first instalment of the 'New Neurotics', which ran from January to March 1999, featured Martin Maloney, Tomoko Takahashi, Steven Gontarski and Brian Cyril Griffiths. While it looked fantastic in the space, there was a widespread feeling that perhaps the bubble had burst.

ADDRESS 98A Boundary Road, London NW8 0RH (0171–624 8299)
OPEN Thursday to Sunday 12.00–18.00
TUBE Swiss Cottage BUS 139

Camden Arts Centre

This red-brick building (now in need of some structural TLC) opened in 1897 as the Hampstead Central Library. In 1965 it was transformed by a group of local artists into a centre for visual arts and has since built a reputation for a wide range of exhibitions and a policy of involving people of all ages in the work, ideas and practices of contemporary artists. Not in this instance PR puff to fulfil increasingly stringent funding criteria – the centre runs one of the most effective education policies of any publicly funded gallery in the capital. Activities include workshops for schools and the community, talks and teachers' evenings inspired by current exhibitions or the many residency schemes and projects in which artists are provided with a studio space or one of the three galleries to make work *in-situ*. Recent talks and events have included a series in association with Cubitt to coincide with the Pride Arts Festival and the gallery's exhibition of work by the Canadian artists' group General Idea, who during their last seven years together turned their attention to the subject of AIDS, producing hundreds of exhibitions, temporary public artworks and projects. In November Scott Heim, writer in residence at the centre in 1998, gave a one-off workshop based on the exhibition of work by Bernd and Hilla Becher, whose photographs of industrial structures such as water towers and pit heads have profoundly influenced post-war European photography. During October and November 1998 Mike Nelson gradually filled gallery III with debris from the street, transforming the detritus into objects and tableaux depicting connections between the original items and their makers.

Marking the end of the building's centenary year and celebrating the start of the centre's North London Link Project, the gallery implemented a series of public works and community projects taking place at sites connected with the North London rail line, the first of which featured

Camden Arts Centre

work by the late Felix Gonzalez Torres, who showed at the gallery in 1994 alongside Ad Reinhardt and Joseph Kosuth. Torres' work, be it a billboard-sized image of an empty unmade bed or a pile of sweets in the corner of the gallery, is always a meeting of the public and private, social and personal. 'Untitled (America)' comprises garlands of lights which were installed between the Centre and the nearby Finchley Road and Frognal railway station.

The centre is the London venue of *New Contemporaries*, the annual showcase of students and recent graduates selected by open submission by a panel of critics, curators and artists. Criticised in recent years for being thin, it has nonetheless given early exposure to the likes of Damien Hirst, Gillian Wearing, and Abigail Lane. The 1998 exhibition, selected by Phyllida Barlow, Eddie Berg, Christine Hohenbuchler and Adrian Searle, featured paintings by Gillian Carnegie and photographs by Sophy Ricketts, both of whom were already familiar to London audiences.

As well as the latest developments, director Jenny Lomax has been unflinching in her desire to focus attention on the work of an older generation. You are as likely to find paintings by Prunella Clough or Patrick Heron as you are new video and photography-based work by Mat Collishaw or Carsten Holler's explorations of the transformative power of art via the potent symbol of the Amanita, familiar to us all as the red and white-spotted mushroom of fairy tales. The gallery also has an excellent bookshop stocking, besides the usual range of exhibition catalogues and periodicals, limited editions by contemporary artists.

ADDRESS Arkwright Road, London NW3 6DG (0171-435 2643)
OPEN Tuesday to Thursday 11.00–19.00, Friday to Sunday 11.00–17.00
TUBE Finchley Road BUS 13, 82

west london

Goethe-Institut Gallery 10.2
Serpentine Gallery 10.4
Lisson Gallery 10.10
Richard Salmon 10.14

Goethe-Institut Gallery

The gallery at the Goethe-Institut opened in 1978 and currently shares the space with a small cafeteria, the noise from which can disrupt viewing. The Institut plans to refurbish all its public rooms by the millennium, after which the gallery will be separate from the café.

Most of its six exhibitions a year are devoted to contemporary German art which, with Berlin fast becoming the city to watch, should raise the profile of an otherwise low-key space. Major exhibitions of the past few years have included works on paper by Gerhard Richter and Dieter Roth, sculpture by Caeseberg, one of the most visible artists of the post-unification period, and large black-and-white photographs by Anna and Bernhard Blume, in which the artists enact bizarre expressionist encounters in a sterile and dying forest.

In November 1998 the gallery showed photographs by Christopher Muller, who has a very formalist approach to subject matter, be it washing up in the sink or a punnet of strawberries.

The 1999 programme includes photographs by Matthias Hoch and by Mona Breede, original book illustrations by Wolf Erlbruch, and a group show of recent work by participants of the visual-arts-scholarship programme of the German Academic Exchange Service. A stronger emphasis on an emerging generation of artists who have not shown before in this country will shape future programmes.

ADDRESS 50 Princes Gate, Exhibition Road, London SW7 2PH (0171-411 3400)
OPEN Monday to Friday 10.00–20.00, Saturday 9.30–12.30
TUBE South Kensington BUS 14, 74, C1

Serpentine Gallery

In 1970 Sue Grayson's idea of transforming a defunct tea pavilion in Kensington Gardens into a space for contemporary art was greeted with deep scepticism. Many believed that its position in a royal park would lead to rigorous restrictions as to the type of work that could be shown – that the gallery would be forced to cater for the passing families and strollers in the park. Initially run by the Arts Council, the Serpentine Gallery in fact had the feel of a fringe space and over the next two decades gained an international reputation with cutting-edge shows by the likes of Allan McCollum and Andrea Schlieker, which, ironically, were popular with the cognoscenti and public alike.

But by 1991, the year Julia Peyton-Jones took over as director, the gallery faced severe problems; there was a significant disparity between its profile and its ability to serve the public and maintain such an ambitious programme. There was no fire alarm or sprinkler system and, because the galleries leaked badly and were hopelessly insecure, collectors and museums were increasingly reluctant to loan works. Peyton-Jones' answer was to launch a hugely ambitious National Lottery bid, eventually securing £3 million of Lottery funding and a further £1 million from private and corporate donors. Architects John Miller and Partners were employed to redesign the Grade-II-listed pavilion and in 1997 the gallery closed for a year of refurbishment.

Even during this period of rebuilding the Serpentine remained active. Artists including Tadashi Kawamata, Rasheed Areen and Anya Gallaccio were invited to create works on the gallery lawn and around the site. A temporary bookshop opened in Warren Street, showing a highly successful series of artists' films.

The revamped Serpentine Gallery opened in spring 1998 and, from the outside at least, looks barely different from the old. The greatest altera-

tions have been carried out beneath the building, where steel piles sunk 4 metres into the earth enabled builders to tunnel beneath the gallery, transforming a shallow space into a functional basement which houses storage and workshops and the plant which controls state-of-the-art lighting and heating controls.

Other benefits include a permanent entrance hall and an enlarged bookshop, capable of remaining open while shows are installed. You now enter from the south side of the building, where a pathway from the road culminates in the first permanent London commission by Ian Hamilton-Finlay – a list, etched in slate, of the Latin names of all the species of tree planted in Hyde Park. Improved lighting and enlarged openings unite what had been four quite disparate spaces. The first gallery, originally a dingy space, boasts a beautiful circular rooflight. The portico in the north gallery has been glazed in to create an education room, which in the summer months houses an artist-in-residence scheme.

The 1998 programme kicked off with a retrospective of Piero Manzoni, famed for canning and selling his own shit and transforming people into living sculptures by allowing them to stand on a specially designed wooden plinth with insoles stuck on top. Manzoni, who died in 1963 at the age of 29, was a true pioneer. A profound influence upon conceptualism, body and performance art, his irreverent humour endures in the work of many young artists today.

Next up came a mid-career retrospective of Cornelia Parker, who in 1995 had attracted large crowds to the Serpentine to see 'The Maybe' which included the actress Tilda Swinton asleep in a glass coffin. Later in the year, the gallery confirmed its commitment to young artists with the techno-Zen 3-D video installations by Mariko Mori and the

Serpentine Gallery

dazzling, elephant-dung-encrusted paintings of 1998 Turner-Prize winner Chris Ofili.

Many have lamented that the idiosyncrasies of the old Serpentine have been ironed out, that, while rain and the burglars can be effectively kept out, charm has given way to institutional anonymity. It is still, however, one of the most beautiful spaces in London, with excellent natural light and extensive views across the park. And, as admission fees to major exhibitions soar, it is worth noting that the Serpentine Gallery is the only publicly funded contemporary-art gallery in London which is free of charge all year round.

ADDRESS Kensington Gardens, London W2 3XA (0171-402 6075)
OPENING TIMES daily 10.00–18.00
TUBE South Kensington BUS 9, 10, 52

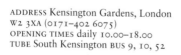

Lisson Gallery

The Lisson Gallery has, in its 30-odd-year history, risen to the highest echelons of the international scene. From student venture to arguably the most respected and revered gallery in London, it has consistently reflected the enthusiasm of its founder Nicholas Logsdail for minimal and conceptual art and their enduring influence upon subsequent generations.

Logsdail started the gallery in his home at 68 Bell Street in 1967 while still a student at the Slade School of Art. Early shows mixed fellow students, including Derek Jarman, with an ambitious line-up of international figures such as Yoko Ono. Logsdail is one of the few British gallerists who can claim truly to have embraced the emergent international trends of minimalism and conceptualism, first bringing to British attention the work of Robert Ryman, Donald Judd, Dan Graham, and Carl Andre, later promoting British artists profoundly influenced by their example.

The Lisson now represents more than 40 artists, from blue-chip minimalist Sol Lewitt, who showed new wall drawings during the summer of 1998, to British artists increasingly dominant in the 1990s: the forensic investigations of 1997 Turner-Prize nominee Christine Borland, the smart word-plays of 1996 nominee Simon Patterson, and the psychologically dark films of the 1996 prize-winner Douglas Gordon have all been shown here during the past few years. But the gallery is perhaps still best known or most readily associated with the generation of 'New-Object' sculptors who emerged in the early 1980s: Tony Cragg, Richard Deacon, Anish Kapoor and Richard Wentworth, most of whom were either nominated for or won the Turner Prize at some point during the decade, and who became known simply as Lisson sculptors.

The gallery itself is world famous architecturally, more akin to a museum than a commercial gallery, or rather a British commercial gallery.

Lisson Gallery

In 1991, during a recession, Logsdail invested more than half a million pounds in a brand new building, linking sites in Lisson and Bell Street and giving architectural substance to the gallery's reputation. Tony Fretton's design is a classic of pared-down purism, with floor-to-ceiling glass panels on the ground and first floors exposing the artworks within. Fretton also wanted to do away with the sense of surveillance felt in many galleries, granting visitors free rein in a series of exhibition spaces whose arrangement allows for small shows to be held concurrently or for larger exhibitions to occupy the entire building.

Lisson remains an indomitable force in the late 1990s. But while Borland, Gordon and Patterson are among the new establishment, Lisson is not a name generally associated with the YBA phenomenon. *Wonderful Life* held in 1993 and the lively *Ideal Standard Summertime* of 1995 mixed the established with new names such as Lucy Gunning, Liam Gillick, and Tim Noble, but few of these were taken up by the gallery.

The 1997/98 programme included work by the late great Donald Judd, Mat Collishaw's videos of hookers shown on silk waterlillies in garden ponds, Avis Newman's slow-revealing 'Meridian' paintings, and the cool one-stroke monochromes of Jason Martin.

ADDRESS 52–54 Bell Street, London NW1 5DA (0171–724 2739)
OPEN Monday to Friday 10.00–18.00, Saturday 10.00–17.00
TUBE Edgware Road BUS 6, 7, 15, 16, 18, 27

Richard Salmon

Just off Kensington High Street lies the monied tranquility of Edwardes Square where, to the south, Richard Salmon enjoys one of the most beautiful galleries in town. The two 10-metre-square first-floor Victorian painting studios overlook the square itself and are flooded with northern light, making almost everything shown look wonderful: from Neil Cummings' museum-style vitrines made from discarded cardboard and filled with a variety of high- and lowbrow objects, to Ken Butler's formal arrangements of potted geraniums, which were shown in September 1998 alongside Damian Elwes' paintings of foliage-filled landscapes, unstretched and hung to create a viewing enclosure.

Since opening in June 1996 the gallery has held a number of ambitious group shows, many of which have toured to public spaces outside London. *Light*, which examined illumination as both psychological sign and physical message, included Marysia Lewandowska's gradually reddening and fading image of an electric hob, and Mariele Neudecker's glass tank containing a model landscape and filled with misty liquid. *Craft* toyed with the multifarious meanings of the word – from derisory to late-1990s hip. Naomi Dines' functionally ambiguous leather harness/sculpture is among the most notable pieces from a show that highlighted the importance of the craftsperson in the realisation of the artist's more wayward ideas; ironically, only Fergal Stapleton and Rebecca Warren owned up to having had someone else construct their sculpture – a beautiful glass rocket.

Through April and May 1998 James Moores showed paintings of weather maps subtitled with daily horoscopes – the meeting of two highly unreliable forecasts. The 1998 programme ended with Markus Eisenmann's immaculate monochrome paintings of shop-front grilles, and everyday objects cast in bronze, then painted to resemble the real thing

Richard Salmon

– the old, reliable frisson of *trompe l'oeil* – and illogical experiments by Morgan Doyle, who divided the gallery by replacing one of the floor-boards with a metal replica, showed a wax model of a rat marooned in a plastic dome and one of the more memorable word pieces of the year: an engraved plaque reading 'Your Presence Annoys Me'.

ADDRESS 59 South Edwardes Square, London W8 6HW (0171–602 9494)
OPEN Tuesday to Saturday 10.30–17.30
TUBE High Street Kensington BUS 9, 10, 27, 28, 31

notting hill

Todd Gallery 11.2
Tablet 11.4

Todd Gallery

Todd Gallery is quite a refuge from Notting Hill's bars, boutiques and trustafarian brigade. Not a particularly stunning gallery but a low-slung single-storey space, ten minutes' walk from the tube, that shows a range of sculpture and painting by slightly older artists who, in the main, favour detail and poetry over bold statements or shock tactics.

Employing a range of pigments, from those used in cave painting to those of the Greek – 'Massicot' – and Italian – 'Naples Yellow' – Maria Lalic paints palimpsests which attempt to contain the whole history of art, the edges of each painting displaying the process like a kind of sedimentary rock. Simon Lewis similarly ignores much of what is going on around him in the art world, creating tiny paintings in oil on gesso on aluminium of impossibly detailed fields and skies. Mark Fairington borrows from the tradition of Dutch flower painting; petals or parts of different flowers float singly or in clusters on glossy black or yellow grounds. Also on show in his 1998 exhibition were photo-realist renditions of mother nature's more *outré* creations – a snail oozing over a cluster of blackberries, a preying mantis enjoying a post-coital snack, a pair of stag beetles locking horns. Mark Pimlott's 1998 installation showed two versions of the 1960s in conflict – the optimism of utopian projects recounted in voice-overs to video images of the many nondescript and socially inadequate buildings that ensued.

ADDRESS 1–5 Needham Road, London W11 (0171–792 1404)
OPEN Wednesday to Friday 11.00–18.00, Saturday 11.00–16.00
TUBE Notting Hill Gate BUS 28, 31, 52

Tablet

The Tabernacle is a multi-purpose centre in Notting Hill. Refurbished with lottery funding, it comprises a performance space, a new-technology centre for young people and is home to various dance and music projects, a café and bar. Kate Macgarry, who with Ben Weaver helped to make Habitat's in-store arts programme such a success, co-ordinates a series of solo exhibitions by contemporary artists in Tablet, The Tabernacle's project-based space to the rear of the building.

Tomoko Takahashi kicked off the programme in spring 1998 with a highly orchestrated installation of office detritus. Des Hughes, one of a growing band of artists inspired by American slacker artist Sean Landers, followed with whimsical and self-deprecating paintings.

In October Yinka Shonibare presented 'Alien Obsessives: Mum, Dad and the Kids' – a family of stuffed-toy aliens covered with African fabric. Shonibare, British-born of African parentage, has described himself as an 'urban primitive' and his works reflect the complexities of post-colonial identity. 1998 was particularly successful for Shonibare. On the night of his opening at The Tabernacle he was one of five artists to win a £30,000 Hamlyn award. Unveiled in the same month was a new commission by INIVA (the Institute of International Visual Arts), a series of staged photographs in which the artist appears in the guise of a nineteenth-century dandy – one of which appeared on poster sites in 50 tube stations across the capital.

ADDRESS The Tabernacle, Powis Square, London W11 2AY (0171-565 7898)
OPEN Thursday to Saturday 12.00–18.00
TUBE Notting Hill Gate/Westbourne Park BUS 31

SW I

White Cube 12.2
Emily Tsingou Gallery 12.6
Institute of Contemporary Arts 12.8
Art Now 12.14

White Cube

As the unofficial headquarters of Young British Art, most famous for being 'Damien Hirst's gallery', White Cube and its director Jay Jopling have enjoyed more column inches than any other space in town. Jopling in fact trades out of an intimate project room designed by acclaimed minimalist architect Claudio Silvestrin. On the first floor of a modest St James Street building, it is surrounded by Old Master galleries and specialist bookshops and sandwiched between Christie's and the Royal Academy.

Jopling started out in the secondary market, flogging minimalism from his Brixton flat. His now-legendary meeting with Hirst occurred in 1991 and Jopling's influence, not to mention his financial skill, cannot be underestimated in the realisation of some of Hirst's more elaborate ideas. Hirst didn't show at the gallery until mid-1995, preceded by YBAs Tracey Emin, Sarah Lucas, and Gavin Turk. Emin responded to Jopling's offer of a show with *My Major Retrospective*, an installation of memorabilia, collages, short stories and drawings, so named because she thought it would be her last.

White Cube's programmes has since oscillated between the fresh-faced – Darren Almond, who in 1997 filled the gallery with an over-sized ceiling fan, was plucked straight from college – and a handful of more established artists such as Mona Hatoum and Anthony Gormley. Hatoum, best known for her 1995 'Corps étranger', an endoscopic and coloscopic journey through her body, showed, in the same year, 'Socle du Monde', a brooding 2-metre steel cube full of magnets and coated with iron filings whose patterns resemble astrakhan.

Besides the well-documented Brit-Art stars, Jopling and co-founder Julia Royse have helped to satisfy the ever-growing appetite for work from the USA. Karen Kilimnik's 1994 installation 'The Legacy' transformed the gallery into a mock-gothic teenage bedroom. White Cube also

White Cube

gave Britain its first taste of Sean Landers, whose slacker posturing and diaristic ramblings have since spawned many a lesser British imitator. Painters Christian Schumann and Caroll Dunham, sculptor Clay Ketter, and the brilliant, category-defying Jessica Stockholder, whose quirky constructions and dishevelled installations stole the show in the first installment of Saatchi's 1998 *Young Americans 2*, have all had solo shows at White Cube in the last couple of years. Terry Winters has floated in and out of fashion for a couple of decades and, after rapturously received exhibitions in New York, showed his densely worked quasi-biological 'Graphic Primitives' paintings in September 1998.

With the lease at Duke Street up for renewal, a move to a larger space in Hoxton Square is on the cards – further fuelling Shoreditch's claim to be the hippest district in the capital.

ADDRESS 44 Duke Street, London SW1Y 6DD (0171–930 5373)
OPEN Friday and Saturday 10.00–18.00
TUBE Green Park BUS 9, 14, 19, 38

Emily Tsingou Gallery

A short walk from White Cube and the ICA and close to Cork Street, the Emily Tsingou Gallery still feels slightly off the beaten gallery track. A small shop-fronted space, it opened in March 1998 with a show of New York-based Karen Kilimnik (briefly a resident at the Delfina Trust studios in Bermondsey). Kilimnik – who had previously shown in London at White Cube and was included in *Belladonna* at the ICA in 1997 – served up a Russian Christmas. Upstairs, her installation featured kitsch paintings, Russian trinkets and fake jewellery on patches of fake snow, cordoned off with ribbon and fairy lights. Downstairs was a more familiar series of drawings of supermodels and stars of pop music and cinema.

In May, the gallery published Henry Bond's *The cult of the street*, an A3-size book of photographs compiled by Joy Division design-guru Peter Saville. In his photographs, Bond stops London in its tracks, freeze-framing fragments of the narratives we glimpse everyday. Both floors of the gallery were filled with more than 200 of these images.

Kilimnik and Bond, while fashionable, were not new to most gallery goers. On the other hand, Peter Pommerer, who showed during August 1998, was a real eye-opener. Barely known outside his native Germany, Pommerer makes richly layered drawings incorporating decorative swirls, stylised flowers, tattoo-like configurations and child-like doodling. Complementing the 20 works on show was a 4-metre-high wall drawing, created in the stairwell that dominates the front of the gallery.

ADDRESS 10 Charles II Street, London SW1Y 4AA (0171–839 5320)
OPEN Tuesday to Saturday 10.00–18.00
TUBE Piccadilly Circus BUS 9, 14, 19, 38

Institute of Contemporary Arts

This elegant John Nash-designed Regency terrace has been home to the ICA since 1967 but the Institute was founded 20 years earlier by a small group of individuals including the poet, critic and champion of modernism Herbert Read and the surrealist painter Roland Penrose. Read envisaged the Institute as 'an adult play centre, where work is a joy, a source of vitality and daring experiment.' Early shows included *Forty Years of Modern Art*, which featured work by Picasso and Bacon.

In its current guise, the ICA has two galleries, a new-media centre, theatre, cinema, cinemathèque, seminar rooms, a bookshop, extensive video and audio archives, a café and bar. Since the introduction in 1968 of the ICA cinema, the institute has given early screenings of films by, among many others, The Brothers Quay, Derek Jarman, and Jan Svankmajer. Luminaries such as Martin Amis, J G Ballard, Jacques Derrida, and Salmon Rushdie, who performed at the ICA theatre in *Shout, Art and Censorship* the night before the Ayatollah issued the *fatwah* against him, have given talks and the live-arts programme has included performances by Laurie Anderson, Annie Sprinkle and The Smiths.

It's not surprising that, in its 50-odd-year history, the Institute has attracted, even courted, its share of controversy. There has been a stabbing on stage (accidental) and a brick through the window (courtesy of Spike Milligan, protesting at an installation which electrocuted goldfish). 1976, the year of the infamous Tate Bricks controversy, was particularly scandalous for the ICA. Mary Kelly's exhibition *Post Partum Document*, which explored the social conditioning of mother and child and featured dirty nappy liners, caused outrage in the press; *Prostitution* by Genesis P Orridge and Cosey Fanni Tutti prompted outbursts by Mary Whitehouse for its use of tampons and pornographic imagery. *Prostitution*

managed to run for just four days – long enough for questions to be raised in Parliament.

In recent years the ICA has shown a wealth of emerging and established talent both from the UK and internationally. Iwona Blazwick (now curator of the Tate Gallery of Modern Art at Bankside) during her period as director of exhibitions gave Damien Hirst his first solo show in a major public gallery in 1992 and initiated a resoundingly successful reappraisal of surrealist Meret Oppenheim. Gary Hume, Siobhan Hapaska, John Currin, and Jake and Dinos Chapman have also benefited from high-profile early-career shows here.

But many now consider the ICA to be less cutting edge than it once was. In 1997, *Assuming Positions*, a mismatched, desperately trendy group show featuring Piotr Uklanski's flashing dance floor and the TV advertisement for blackcurrant Tango, drew widespread scorn. In a rare attack, *Time Out* critic Sarah Kent suggested that if this was the best the Institute could do to celebrate its fiftieth anniversary, then perhaps it was time for it to close.

Has it bounced back? The jury is still out. Late 1998 saw two relatively traditional shows back to back. *Surfacing* examined the resurgence of drawing among young artists such as Paul Noble, who in large-scale obsessive drawings continues to detail his urban creation 'Nobson Newtown', and Emma Kay, who draws endearingly imperfect maps from memory. *Die Young Stay Pretty*, curated by and including work by the omnipresent Martin Maloney, celebrated skill, craft and decoration with the op-art and text paintings of Peter Davies, Dexter Dalwood's painterly forays into places he has never been, and Michael Raedecker's paintings which are garnished with patches of stitching and embroidery.

There is now much speculation as to whether the ICA will leave its

Institute of Contemporary Arts

current premises. Anxious to embrace an emerging generation of artists who are seeking different ways of locating and presenting their work, the Institute wants to commission a new building which will challenge the relationships between space, artist and public, with flexibility as a primary objective. Feasibility studies into the proposed move are currently underway.

ADDRESS The Mall, London SW1Y 5AH (0171–930 3647)
OPEN Saturday to Thursday 12.00–19.30, Friday 12.00–17.00
TUBE Charing Cross BUS 3, 6, 9, 11, 12, 13, 15, 15B, X15, 24, 29, 53, 53X, 77A, 88, 109, 139, 159, 176, 177, 196 to Trafalgar Square

Art Now

In the absence of a space dedicated solely to contemporary art, in 1995 the Tate Gallery initiated Art Now, a specially designed projects room towards the rear of the ground floor of the building. Art Now houses a changing programme of five exhibitions a year, including work by both new and established artists from the UK and abroad. In its first year the space confirmed the Tate's commitment to broadening the range of art shown, with 'OTTOshaft', American artist Matthew Barney's installation of strange objects and video images, Marc Quinn's 'Emotional Detox', a series of lead body casts inspired by the seven deadly sins, and 'Broken Mirror', a glass-and-sound sculpture by the French-Canadian artist Geneviéve Cadieux.

The 1996 programme included Georgina Starr's frenetic installation 'Hypnodreamdruff' and Paul Graham's 'Hypermetropia', a series of photographs taken in response to Japan's relentless urban development. With the aim of reaching Mount Fuji, Graham moved in a straight line from his apartment in north-east Tokyo, picking out a high building through his viewfinder and walking to it in order to take the next photograph – Mount Fuji remained a point on the horizon that was never reached. From May to August 1997, Israeli-born artist Michal Rovner filled three walls of the darkened room with video screens, each showing birds swarming to a soundtrack of aircraft, rotorblades and distant gunfire. Swiss artist Beat Streuli followed with photographs of the anonymous crowds on Oxford Street, projected on a huge scale, cross-faded and overlapped to create an oddly beautiful version of the usual hateful experience.

Sophie Calle is still best known for her 'Suite Venitienne' series of photographs, taken in 1980, of a man spotted in a Paris crowd whom she eventually trailed to Venice and back. During the summer of 1998

she presented her first major sculptural installation, 'The Birthday Cere-mony'. Over a period of 14 years starting in 1980, Calle held an annual dinner party to celebrate her birthday, matching the number of guests to her age. The gifts she received were placed in a cabinet, the contents replaced each year, and replicas of the original cabinet, each filled with presents, were shown in the gallery – more a *memento mori* than a cele-bration of life.

From September to October 1998, following on from 'The Nam', her fast-paced description of scenes from Vietnam films, Fiona Banner trans-formed the car-chase scene from Kathryn Bigelow's 1991 film *Point Break* into an arresting landscape of words, recounting frame by frame the build up of momentum in hazard-red marker pen on a giant canvas.

What Art Now proves is the need for a consistent showcase for contem-porary artists in our public museums. For this, we will have to wait for the Tate Gallery of Art, Bankside, due for completion in 2000.

ADDRESS Tate Gallery, Millbank, London SW1P 4RG (0171–887 8000)
OPEN daily 10.00–17.30
TUBE Pimlico BUS C10, 77A

seı

Hayward Gallery 13.2
Jerwood Gallery 13.6
Delfina 13.10

Hayward Gallery

The Hayward Gallery, a classic example of brutalist architecture, opened in 1968. Part of the concrete sprawl that is the South Bank Centre, it has been the subject of much criticism but, vitally, has proved to be one of the most important and flexible spaces in the capital, able to adapt to suit the wide range of contemporary and historical shows staged during its 30-year history.

From Rodin to Tatsuo Miyajima, Renoir to Robert Mapplethorpe, the Hayward has brought a diverse programme to a wide audience. In 1998 alone, exhibitions of Henri Cartier-Bresson, Francis Bacon, Bruce Nauman, and Anish Kapoor were held. Cartier-Bresson and Bacon were shown concurrently, offering an astonishing juxtaposition of talent and temperament by near contemporaries. Nauman's cryptic neon word-and-video pieces, executed with devastating humour, proved him to be one of the masters of contemporary art and a profound influence on recent generations of British artists. The galleries have rarely looked better than for the Kapoor exhibition: sculptures set into the wall or floor plunged into seemingly bottomless holes or exquisitely coloured limitless voids. 'On the Edge of the World' filled an entire gallery, funnelling up towards a red/black immensity. But the most affecting piece was also one of the smallest: 'Ghost', a slab of limestone sliced on one side, contains an aperture that reflects both the light of the gallery and the form of the viewer, flickering like a phantom projection just in front of the solid.

Well-curated surveys offering fresh perspectives on historical themes and artistic movements have been *Gravity and Grace*, a beautifully installed review of minimalism and its legacy, and *Material Culture*, which traced developments in British sculpture defined by the ways in which artists refer to or redefine objects. Most recently, *Addressing the Century: 100 years of art and fashion* explored the way in which key

figures from the worlds of art and fashion have contributed to some of this century's most radical innovations, highlighting moments when the two disciplines have converged and featuring clothes by Issey Miyake and sculpture by Mona Hatoum.

Expansive approaches to contemporary painting by the likes of Peter Doig, Jonathan Lasker, Jessica Stockholder, and relative newcomer Zebedee Jones were seen in *Unbound: Possibilities in Painting*, curated by Greg Hilty and Adrian Searle in 1995. Art of non-Western cultures featured in 1997's *Rhapsodies in Black: Art of the Harlem Renaissance* and in the 1999 exhibition *Cities on the Move*.

National Touring Exhibitions, managed by the Hayward on behalf of the Arts Council, annually brings around 30 shows to 1.4 million people in more than 100 venues all over Britain, from major museums to colleges and libraries. The Arts Council Collection, which was started in 1946, now contains more than 7000 works. A selection of the most recent acquisitions – such as Richard Patterson's painting of an enlarged toy, 'Motocrosser', Tania Kovats' full-scale model of a 'Grotto', and Hadrian Piggot's 'Instrument of Hygiene', a washbasin set into a suitcase for travelling neurotics – were shown in *ACE!* in 1996.

Since 1970 the gallery's neon tower, designed by Philip Vaughan and Roger Dainton, has been a landmark. A more recent addition is the barn-like construction, designed by Allies and Morrison, grafted on to one of the sculpture balconies overlooking Waterloo Bridge; it houses the café.

ADDRESS South Bank Centre, London SE1 8XX (0171–960 5226)
OPEN daily 10.00–18.00
TUBE Waterloo BUS 1, D1, 4, P11, 26, 68, 76, 77, 149, 168, 171, 176, 188, 211, 501, 505, 507

Jerwood Gallery

The Jerwood Foundation supports theatre, dance and other arts groups and individuals through grants and its prestigious annual prizes. Addressing the need for practical help, in 1996 the Foundation purchased a four-storey former Victorian school in Southwark with the aim of converting it into low-cost rehearsal and production facilities for young drama and dance practitioners together with a gallery space for emerging artists.

The conversion was made possible by a grant of £1.4 million from the Arts Council's National Lottery Fund awarded in 1997 and the long-awaited Jerwood Space, converted by architects Paxton Locher, opened in September 1998. A new resource both for Foundation beneficiaries and the commercial sector such as West-End-theatre producers, television- and film-production companies, graphic and fashion designers, the Space combines rehearsal studios and dedicated production offices, some available for hire, a café, and an excellent new art gallery for the capital.

The Jerwood Gallery, which opens on to Union Street, incorporates elements of the original structure with three connecting spaces amounting to more than 240 square metres with access to an external sculpture space. Stephen Hepworth – formerly director of The Tannery in Bermondsey, one of London's largest alternative spaces where he raised the profile and curated shows including established artists such as Paul McCarthy, Mariko Mori and Georgina Starr – is in charge of a year-round programme of work by emerging artists which began in November 1998 with *dumbpop*. Included in this group show of good-humoured and optimistic work by artists largely in their twenties were Ana Genoves, who in her three-dimensional work freeze-frames natural forms – a puddle with concentric rings caused by splashes of rain, for example – trans-

Jerwood Gallery

forming the fleeting into the meditative, and Philippe Pareno, whose inflated cartoon speech bubbles floated free in the gallery.

The inaugural show, however, was the annual Jerwood Painting Prize, which in its fifth year finally found a permanent home. The Jerwood Prize is always a mixed bag. Notable not least for the £30,000 received by the winner, it is perhaps the only prize that pits emerging painters against their elders – no bad thing. The 1998 exhibition of shortlisted artists included strong works by Edwina Leapman and Basil Beattie, both in their sixties, as well as the dizzying, dotted and elephant-dung-studded canvases of young star Chris Ofili, and elegant paintings combining images of butterflies and diagrams of the human brain by winner Madeleine Strindberg.

The Jerwood Gallery will undoubtedly draw a large audience. In a part of Southwark that is fast developing, it is close to both the Globe Theatre and the new Tate Gallery of Modern Art at Bankside and is a five-minute walk from Borough tube station and ten minutes from Waterloo.

ADDRESS Jerwood Space, 171 Union Street, London SE1 0LN (0171-654 0171)
OPEN Monday to Sunday 10.00–18.00
TUBE Borough, Waterloo BUS 21, 35, 133 to Borough 4, 26, 68, 68A, 76, 168, 176, 188, 211 to Waterloo

Delfina

Delfina Entrecanales has been described as a fairy godmother to young artists. In 1988 the septagenarian philanthropist founded the Delfina Trust which provides free studio space and accommodation for nine-month periods to foreign artists and offers a free studio to British artists for up to two years. Its current residence, a large red-brick building in Bermondsey Street, close to London Bridge station, houses the studio complex and an impressive exhibition space which, under the directorship of David Gilmour, stages four shows a year, alternating between British and international artists. Delfina is run as a public space, with no commission taken on work shown and no admission fee charged to the public. It also boasts an excellent café (the labels for the house wine have been specially designed by Mark Wallinger) which is open for lunch but closed at weekends.

In recent years the Trust seems to have upgraded its intake from fresh-faced graduates to names already well known on the international circuit. The list of 1998–99 residents includes Maureen Gallace, who is represented in New York by the super-trendy 303 gallery and showed her subdued paintings of the Connecticut landscape at Interim Art in 1998, and Thomas Demand, another 303 artist who shows in London with the Victoria Miro Gallery. Demand's large-scale photographs depict anonymous unpopulated interior and architectural details which, on closer inspection, turn out to be immaculately constructed mock-ups built from paper and cardboard of such eerie places as Jeffrey Dahmer's apartment. In 1998 Demand was nominated for the prestigious Citibank Private Bank Photography Prize.

There is no obligation for resident artists to show in Delfina's gallery space but not surprisingly many do so. 1998 was a particularly strong year for the gallery. During March and April, Anya Gallaccio, famed for

Delfina

her installations using organic matter such as ice or bright red gerberas, used thousands of glass crystals that acted as tiny prisms to create a luminous rainbow in the darkened space. From May to July the gallery was filled with Manuel Ocampo's environment of paintings in the form of hammocks, cushions and carpets. Ridiculing the values attributed to Art and Culture, Ocampo invited viewers to walk, sit, or even sleep on his paintings. In October, Mark Wallinger, who was nominated for the 1995 Turner Prize, presented 'The Four Corners of the Earth', in which slides of a small globe were projected on to canvas to become convincingly three-dimensional.

ADDRESS 50 Bermondsey Street, London SE1 3UD (0171-357 6600)
OPEN Monday to Friday 10.00–17.00, Saturday and Sunday 14.00–17.00
TUBE London Bridge BUS P4, 21, 35, 48, 133 to London Bridge

south london

Gasworks 14.2
Beaconsfield 14.4
Milch 14.6
South London Gallery 14.8
Museum of Installation 14.12
Hales Gallery 14.16

Gasworks

One of several artist-studio complexes to have an attached gallery, Gasworks aims to provide a 'first outing' for young artists as well as an experimental space for the more established. In addition, it runs a programme for visiting artists from as far afield as Cuba, Kenya and India, who each are given the opportunity to work for up to three months in one of three allotted studios and have an exhibition or open studio, often their first in this country, at the end of their residency.

SAD, held in January 1997 as a follow up to the inaugural show DAD, was a diverse mixture of students and well-known names such as John Stezaker, Jenny Saville, and Tracey Emin. The blend is usually more even, with emergent talent filling most of the short-run exhibitions held each year. *Insulator* featured intensely drawn aerial views of environments and landscapes by Chad McCail, now represented by Laurent Delaye Gallery. Others to gain early exposure include Elisa Sighicelli, whose back-lit photographic images of evocative empty interiors were shown in February 1998 and, later in the year, at Laure Genillard Gallery. During September 1998 Andrew Moszynski created a wall-painting based on graphic devices used in advertising. In November, *Eliminate the Negative* included paintings by Donny Rolph, Jo Bruton, and Jane Harris.

ADDRESS 155 Vauxhall Street, London SE11 5RH (0171–735 3445)
OPEN Friday to Sunday 12.00–18.00
TUBE Oval BUS 36, 185

Beaconsfield

David Crawford and Naomi Siderfin began Nosepaint, an organisation dedicated to the promotion of performance art and time-based events, in the early 1990s, holding one-off events in various locations including the Ministry of Sound and St Thomas' Hospital. Beaconsfield is a more conventional venue; a former 'ragged school' at the west end of the river-side walk which leads to the South Bank Centre. But, one of the more ambitious artist-led organisations in London, it has collaborated with artists and organisations at home and abroad, staged concerts by young British composers and performers and presented 'w.a.f.s.', a film by Keith Coventry. In December 1997, Tomoko Takahashi worked with composer Neill Quinton, responding to the 'visual music' she perceived in the space. Walking around the installation of high-tech office detritus, viewers were offered an acoustiguide and a tape of piano music.

Themed group shows in this large exhibition space, with uniquely sloping wooden floor and rickety balcony, have included 'Maps Else-where' co-curated with the Institute of International Visual Arts (inIVA), *Rax*, the first gathering of contemporary Finnish art in London, and *Glean*, in which artists were asked to draw inspiration from the local area and create works *in situ*. Anna Best hung glitterballs beneath a walkway and provided a chalkboard for residents and visitors to write comments. Keith Coventry presented a collection of home-made crack-pipes and a blank canvas. New paintings by Mikey Cuddihy were shown in December 1998, followed by a multimedia commission including a publication, CD and video by Orphan Drift and Ccru.

ADDRESS Newport Street, London SE11 6AY (0171–582 6465)
OPEN Friday to Sunday 12.00–18.00
TUBE Vauxhall BUS 77, 344

Milch

First run by the late Lawren Maben, Milch has given early exposure to Douglas Gordon, Simon Patterson, and Sarah Staton, best known for her 'Supastore', a collection of artists' multiples and pseudo-commodities originally shown at Laure Genillard Gallery in 1995. In 1996 Milch was re-established as an independent arts charity under the directorship of Lisa Panting and Fred Mann and moved from Bloomsbury to a series of wonderfully crumbling subterranean spaces close to Centre Point in Charing Cross Road. One of the few truly alternative spaces in central London, the gallery was a superb venue for diverse and challenging work such as Jane and Louise Wilson's 1997 video 'Crawl Space', and 'I Beg to Differ' in which 20 artists' films fought for attention.

Milch is currently on the first floor of a converted warehouse, a less idiosyncratic space directly across the river from the Tate. The new programme opened with *Anthem*, an exploration of differing Westernised attitudes towards national and corporate identity featuring commissioned works by Jonathan Parsons and a first UK presentation of young American artist Neil Goldberg. Since 1994 Goldberg has been anonymously faxing details of his dreams to US corporations and presented a wall full of these bizarre, often incoherent texts. Parsons showed a series of national flags, their colours reduced to harmonising tones of black and brown. The 1999 programme includes a second solo show of Kate Davies' poetically ruminative sculptures and a group exhibition that will draw from the worlds of art and fashion design. Milch also plans to produce a CD of experimental music, interviews and sound works by artists.

ADDRESS 2–10 Tinworth Street, London SE11 5EH (0171-735 7334)
OPEN Thursday to Sunday 12.00–18.00
TUBE Vauxhall BUS 2, 12, 36, 77, 344

Milch

South London Gallery

A dowdy local gallery has been transformed into one of London's foremost venues, a cathedral of a space. Built in 1891 with the aim of bringing art to one of the most impoverished areas of the capital, the gallery is a huge, high-ceilinged, top-lit space – one of the few that can fully adapt to suit the many and varied media used by artists today, the best of whom director David Thorp has brought to SE5 with limited funding by the London Borough of Southwark and support from grants and external funding bodies and commercial sponsors.

Guest curators have included Carl Freedman, whose 1995 show *Minky Manky* reassembled, five years on from the seminal showcases *Modern Medicine* and *Gambler*, YBAs Damien Hirst, Tracey Emin, and Mat Collishaw. *Popoccultural* organised by the Cabinet Gallery in 1997, gave Americans Jason Fox, Ellen Cantor, and Jeffrey Vallance their first UK museum show alongside the homegrown talent of Chris Ofili and Paul Noble. In the same year, *Some Kind of Heaven*, curated by Eva Meyer-Hermann and Sadie Coles, brought together the work of some of the more prominent women artists working today and included Georgina Starr's comic book filled with molestors and murderers, Mariko Mori's photographic self-portraits as mermaid, pop star and space captain and, best of all, Sylvie Fleury's giant rockets covered in fake fur to resemble cavemen and titled 'First Spaceship on Venus'.

Recent years have seen important solo shows including Bill Viola's video installation 'The Messenger', Gilbert and George's *Naked Shit Pictures*, Brian Catling's 'Cyclops' video projection, and new paintings by Anselm Kiefer. In March 1998, Marc Quinn, best-known for 'Self', the sculpture made from pints of his own blood frozen into the shape of his head, gave a virtuoso display of ideas, techniques and materials including 'Across the Universe', a life-sized self-portrait in ice, and

'Bleached', a banana skin peeled back to reveal the imprint of a human form. *Lovecraft*, held during April and May, celebrated obsessive and decorative work by Lily van der Stokker, Russell Crotty and Udomsak Krisanamis. Gavin Turk's major solo exhibition through September and October included smart art-historical references such as a urinal signed by the artist (after Duchamp), a bronze of a paint roller (after Manzoni) and a sculptural version of David's 'Death of Marat', with Turk playing Marat in his bath. The year ended with *Site Construction*, a group show of young artists working in Berlin, a city tipped by some to be the new 'art capital'.

ADDRESS 65 Peckham Road, London SE5 8UH (0171–703 6120)
OPEN Tuesday to Friday 11.00–18.00, Thursday 11.00–19.00, Saturday and Sunday 14.00–18.00
TUBE Elephant & Castle then BUS 171, 12 or P3, or TUBE Oval then BUS 36

Museum of Installation

The name might seem a contradiction in terms but the Museum of Installation, founded in 1990 by Nicola Oxley, Nicolas De Oliveira and Michael Petry, is dedicated to the research and production of installation and site-specific commissions. A registered charity that operates on project funding via bodies such as the Arts Council of England, the London Arts Board and the Henry Moore Foundation, it has successfully initiated more than 60 different projects at its own premises and on sites on mainland Europe and in the United States.

Initially based in Great Sutton Street, where commissions by Phyllida Barlow, Rob Kessler, Ron Haselden, and Renato Niemis were shown, in 1997 the Museum of Installation acquired the former retail premises in Deptford High Street that now house their office, archive and a range of project-based spaces. Opening the new space was *Musée Imaginaire*, a two-part show in which artists were invited to address real and imagined museums. In response, Terry Smith took a Hoover to London's principal homes of contemporary art, such as the Tate Gallery, and cleaned their administration offices, attaching the fluff he acquired to the wall in a neat A4 rectangle. The dank basement was cleaned and the walls coated with coconut butter by Nathaniel Stewart and, on the ground floor, a reading room contained more than 100 identical cardboard boxes which were sent to artists, writers, architects and curators to be filled, a reference to similar projects initiated by Fluxus and surrealist artists.

The 1998 programme began with *Mercury*, installations by six male artists including Dermot O' Brien and Gordon Dawson – a companion piece to the preceding exhibition, *Mirror*, which featured six women artists. In November, Carl von Weiler attached TV monitors to the ceiling of the basement, each of which showed footage of the artist

hanging upside-down, an echo of the endurance feats of 1970s' performance artists.

Since its inception the Museum of Installation has begun to compile the first major archive on installation, the outcome of which has been the book *Installation Art*, published by Thames & Hudson.

ADDRESS 175 Deptford High Street, London SE8 3NU (0181–692 8778)
OPEN Tuesday to Friday 12.00–17.00, Saturday 14.00–17.00
BR Deptford BUS 47, 53

Hales Gallery

One of the more permanent fixtures of the independent scene, since 1992 Hales has provided a platform for many young British artists including the Chapman brothers, Sarah Jones, and John Frankland. Situated in Deptford High Street close to the Museum of Installation (see page 14.12), it proves that an unlikely and not altogether easily accessible venue can still attract major collectors. On the ground floor, serving both the local bohemia and traders from the market outside, the gallery runs an excellent café, the profits from which fund many of the shows in the basement exhibition space. As a result, gallery artists are given a level of creative freedom not afforded them by many commercial galleries reliant on sales, or artist-run spaces with no real financial support.

Notable successes include solo shows by Tomoko Takahashi, Keith Wilson, and Ian Dawson, all included in the recent Saatchi publication, *The New Neurotic Realism*. Martin McGinn, who won the EAST International '98 Prize, derives his paintings from photographs of artificial light sources, stripping away extraneous detail to leave, for example, a solitary light bulb on a neutral ground. Claude Heath, whose drawings are blindfold explorations of people and objects, and David Leapman, who makes psychedelic paintings of metamorphic objects, were both shortlisted for the 1998 Jerwood Painting Prize.

ADDRESS 70 Deptford High Street, London SE8 4RT (0181-694 1194)
OPEN Monday to Saturday 10.00–16.00
BR Deptford BUS 53, 172

index

Index

ACME 1.10, 1.24, 1.30
Agency, The **2.10–2.12**
Allies and Morrison 13.4
Amis, Martin 12.8
Anderson O'Day 1.28
Andrew Mummery Gallery 1.28, **3.4**
Annely Juda Fine Art **6.10–6.12**
Anthony d'Offay Gallery **6.2–6.4**, 6.6, 8.8
Anthony Reynolds Gallery **6.6–6.8**
Anthony Wilkinson Fine Art 1.24, **1.28**
Approach, The **1.22**, 1.24, 5.16
Art Monthly 5.12
Art Now (Tate Gallery) 0.3, 6.6, **12.14–12.16**
Arts Council Collection 13.4
Arts Council of England 10.4, 13.4, 13.6, 14.12
Asprey, Charles 5.16
Asprey Jacques 0.1, 2.4, **5.16**
Atlantic Bar & Grill, The 8.8

Ballard, J G 12.8
Banner, Fiona 7.2
Barlow, Phyllida 9.10
Beaconsfield 0.1, **14.4**
Berg, Eddie 9.10
Bernard Jacobson Gallery 0.3
Bigelow, Kathryn 12.16
Bill, Simon 2.2
Blair, Tony 0.2
Blazwick, Iwona 12.10
Bow Arts Trust 1.8
Burchill, Julie 8.4

Cabinet Gallery 0.3, 14.8
Camden Arts Centre 4.10
Camerawork **1.20**
Cargill, Duncan 4.6
Cave, Nick 8.2
Ccru 14.4
Chapman Fine Arts 8.8
Chisenhale Gallery **1.16–1.18**, 1.24, 1.30, 5.10
Citibank Private Bank Photography Prize 5.6, 7.12, 5.10
City Racing 0.3
'Cleveland' 4.10
Coast 8.8
Coles, Sadie 8.8, 14.8
Corvi Mora, Tommaso 4.2
Crawford, David 14.4
Cubitt Gallery 1.28

d'Offay, Anthony 6.2
Dainton, Roger 13.4
Delfina 0.1, **13.10–13.12**
Delfina Trust 12.6, 13.10
De Oliveira, Nicolas 14.12
Derrida, Jacques 12.8
Deutsch Britische Freundschaft 2.4
Duncan Cargill Gallery **4.6**

Eagle Gallery, The 1.28
EAST International Prize 14.16
Emily Tsingou Gallery **12.6**
Entrecanales, Delfina 13.10
Entwistle 0.1, **5.12–5.14**
Exhibitions
    ACE! 13.4

Index

Exhibitions (continued)

Addressing the Century: 100 years of art and fashion 13.2
Alice 1.8
Anthem 14.6
Assuming Positions 12.10
Aurifiction and Aurifaction 1.8
A–Z 1.22
Backspace 1.14
Belladonna 12.6
British Figurative Art 1.32
BT *New Contemporaries* 4.10
Cities on the Move 13.4
Cloth-Bound 3.2
Cluster Bomb 2.4
Craft 10.14
DAD 14.2
De Dam 7 Mei 7.10
Die Young Stay Pretty 5.20, 12.10
Dissolution 8.2
Dissolution: Made in the USA 8.2
Documenta, Kassel 5.12
Documenta X, Kassel 5.22
Don't Hate, Sculpt 1.18
dumbpop 13.6
Eliminate the Negative 14.2
Forty Years of Modern Art 12.8
Freeze 0.0, 9.4
From Figure to Object 7.2
Gambler 14.8
Glean 14.4
God 6.6
Gravity and Grace 13.2
Ideal Standard Summertime 10.12
Insulator 14.2

Law, The 8.8
Light 10.14
Lovecraft 14.10
Material Culture 13.2
Mayday in the Global Nursery 7.10
Mercury 14.12
Minky Manky 14.8
Modern Medicine 14.8
Musée Imaginaire 14.12
My Major Retrospective 12.2
Naked Shit Pictures 14.8
New Contemporaries 9.4, 9.10
New Neurotic Realism, The 0.2, 5.12, 9.6
Non-Objective World 1914–18, The 6.10
NWUK 1.18
Origin of Parties, The 4.8
Out 7.6
Pals and Chums 1.20
Popoccultural 14.8
Portraits of People Who Never Existed 5.12
Post Partum Document 12.8
Preview 7.6
Prostitution 12.8
Rax 14.4
Rhapsodies in Black: Art of the Harlem Renaissance 13.4
SAD 14.2
Sensation 5.16, 8.2, 9.4
Sightings 4.8
Site Construction 14.10
Some Kind of Heaven 14.8
Speed 1.4, 7.10

Index

Exhibitions (continued)
Stepping Out 3.4
Stepping Up 3.4
Still 8.2
Surfacing 12.10
Thirties, The 6.10
Turning the Tables 1.18
2in1(x4+1) 1.6
Unbound: Possibilities in Painting 5.10, 13.4
Venice Biennale 7.2
Whitechapel Open 1.4
Wonderful Life 10.12
Young Americans 7.6, 9.4
Young Americans 2 5.4, 8.8, 12.4
Young British Artists III 8.2
Young Germans 9.4
Young Internationals 1.4

Flash Art 2.4
Flowers East **1.32**
Fluxus 2.14
Freedman, Carl 14.8
Fretton, Tony 10.12
Friedman, Stephen 5.20
Frieze 5.12
Frith Street Gallery **7.2–7.4**

Gasworks **14.2**
Genillard, Laure 3.2
Gilmour, David 13.10
Glen Dimplex Award 1.12
Goethe-Institut Gallery **10.2**
Goldsmiths' College 0.0, 1.12, 2.4, 5.8, 5.12, 6.8, 8.2

Gordon, Max 6.10, 9.2
Graham Paton Gallery 1.32
Grassi, Cornelia 4.8, 4.10
Grayson, Sue 10.4
Greengrassi **4.8**

Habitat 11.4
Hales Gallery 0.1, **14.16**
Hamlyn, Jane 7.2
Hamlyn awards 11.4
Hayward Gallery 5.10, **13.2–13.4**
Heller, Margot 6.2
Henrietta House 1.28
Henry Moore Foundation 14.12
Hepworth, Stephen 13.6
Hilty, Greg 13.4
Hohenbuchler, Christine 9.10
Home, Nathaniel 7.2
Hyde Park 10.6

ICA, *see* Institute of Contemporary Arts
inIVA, *see* Institute of International Visual Arts
Installation Art 14.14
Institute of Contemporary Arts 2.14, 4.8, 5.12, 5.20, 12.6, **12.8–12.12**
Institute of International Visual Arts 11.4, 14.4
Interim Art 1.18, 1.24, **1.30**, 13.10

Jacques, Alison 5.16
Jerwood Foundation 13.6
Jerwood Gallery 2.4, **13.6–13.8**
Jerwood Painting Prize 1.4, 13.8, 14.16
John Miller and Partners 10.4

Index

John Moores Prize 3.2, 5.2

Jopling, Jay 12.2

Karsten Schubert Gallery 4.10, 5.10, 6.2, 7.2, 7.6

Kensington Gardens 10.4, 10.8

Kent, Sarah 1.18, 12.10

Klassnik, Robin 1.10

Laure Genillard Gallery **3.2**, 14.2, 14.6

Laurent Delaye Gallery 1.28, **8.2–8.4**, 14.2

LEA Gallery, see Lux Gallery

Lisson Gallery **10.10–10.12**

Logsdail, Nicholas 10.10, 10.12

Lomax, Jenny 9.10

London Arts Board 1.16, 1.24, 14.12

London Electronic Arts, see LEA Gallery

London Filmmakers' Co-op 2.6

London Projects **7.6–7.8**

Lotta Hammer **4.10–4.12**

Lux Centre 2.8

Lux Gallery **2.6–2.8**

Maben, Lawren 14.6

Macgarry, Kate 11.4

McGowan, Martin 0.3

Magnani, Gregorio 4.2

Maloney, Martin 5.20

Mann, Fred 14.6

Marc Jancou Gallery 7.6

Marlborough Gallery 0.3

Mash 8.8

Matt's Gallery **1.10–1.14**

Meyer-Hermann, Eva 14.8

Michael Hue-Williams **5.6**

Milch **14.6**

Millar, Jeremy 1.4

Miller, Jake 1.22

Milligan, Spike 12.8

Miro, Victoria 5.2

Miyake, Issey 13.4

Modern Art !nc **2.2**

Modern Review, The 8.4

Momart 1.32

Morrison Judd **2.4**

Muir, Gregor 2.6

Mulsion, Matt E 1.10

Mummery, Andrew 3.4

Museum of Installation 0.1, 3.4, **14.12–14.14**

Nash, John 12.8

National Lottery 1.8, 10.4, 11.4, 13.6

Natwest Painting Prize 7.2

Nesbitt, Judith 1.16

New Neurotic Realism, The 1.34, 5.12, 9.4, 14.16

North London Link Project 9.8

Nosepaint 14.4

Notting Hill 11.2, 11.4

Nunnery, The **1.8**

Ogg, Kirsty 1.26

One in the Other **1.6**

Orphan Drift 14.4

Oxley, Nicola 14.12

Paley, Maureen 1.18, 1.30

Panting, Lisa 14.6
Paton, Graham 1.34
Paton Gallery **1.34**
Paxton Locher 13.6
Penrose, Roland 12.8
Petry, Michael 14.12
Peyton-Jones, Julia 10.4
Phillips, Gregory 5.20
Photographers' Gallery, The 5.6, **7.10–7.12**
Pride Arts Festival 9.8

Ray, Charles 1.30
Read, Herbert 12.8
Renton, Andrew 4.10
Reynolds, Anthony 6.8
Reynolds, Sir Joshua 7.2
Richard Salmon **10.14–10.16**
Ridinghouse Editions 5.16
Robert Prime **4.2–4.4**
Roberts, John 1.20
Royal Academy of Arts 0.2, 0.3, 5.16, 9.4
Royal Festival Hall 1.28
Royse, Julia 12.2
Rushdie, Salmon 12.8

Saatchi, Charles 0.0, 0.2, 1.22, 1.28, 1.34, 5.12, 9.2–9.4
Saatchi Gallery 0.1, 1.8, 1.10, 5.4, 7.6, 8.2, 8.8, **9.2–9.6**, 12.4
Sadie Coles HQ **8.8–8.10**
Saville, Peter 12.6
Searle, Adrian 9.10, 13.4
Serpentine Gallery 1.28, **10.4–10.8**

Shave, Stuart 2.2
Shoreditch 2.2, 12.4
Shout, Art and Censorship 12.8
Showroom, The **1.24–1.26**
Siderfin, Naomi 14.4
Silvestrin, Claudio 12.2
Sladen, Mark 12.4
Slade School of Art 10.10
Smiths, The 12.8
Southampton Art Gallery 1.28
South Bank Centre 13.2, 13.4
South London Gallery **14.8–14.10**
Sprinkle, Annie 12.8
Stephen Friedman Gallery 0.1, **5.20–5.22**
Stigter, Gerard 6.6
Streets, etc
    Approach Road 1.22
    Arkwright Road 9.10
    Barrett Street 8.4
    Beck Road 1.30
    Bell Street 10.10, 10.12
    Bermondsey Street 0.1, 13.10, 13.12
    Bonner Road 1.24, 1.26
    Boundary Road 9.6
    Bow Road 1.8
    Brick Lane 8.8
    Bruton Place 8.6
    Cambridge Heath Road 1.28
    Charles II Street 2.6
    Charlotte Road 2.10, 2.12
    Chisenhale Road 1.18
    Clerkenwell Road 3.2
    Cleveland Street 4.12
    Clifford Street 5.16, 5.18
    Copperfield Road 1.10, 1.14

Index

Streets, etc (continued)
  Cork Street 0.1, 5.4, 5.6, 5.8, 5.10, 5.14, 12.6
  Deptford High Street 0.1, 14.12, 14.14, 14.16
  Dering Street 6.2, 6.4, 6.8, 6.12
  Duke Street 12.4
  Edwardes Square 10.14, 10.16
  Exhibition Road 10.2
  Fashion Street 5.2, 8.8
  Fitzroy Street 4.8, 4.10
  Foley Street 4.10, 7.6
  French Place 2.4
  Frith Street 7.4, 7.6, 7.8
  Great Newport Street 7.10, 7.12
  Great Ormond Street 1.28
  Great Sutton Street 3.4
  Grove Road 1.16
  Heddon Street 8.10
  Hoxton Square 0.1, 2.6, 2.8, 12.4
  Mall, The 12.12
  Martello Street 1.10
  Millbank 12.16
  Needham Road 11.2
  Newport Street 14.4
  Old Burlington Street 5.20, 5.22
  Old Street 0.1
  Peckham Road 14.10
  Powis Square 11.4
  Princes Gate 10.2
  Redchurch Street 2.2
  Richmond Road 1.32, 1.34
  Roman Road 1.20
  St Christopher's Place 8.4
  St John's Street 8.8
  Shoreditch High Street 2.2, 2.4
  Tenter Ground 1.6
  Tinworth Street 14.6
  Underwood Street 2.16
  Union Street 13.6, 13.8
  Vauxhall Street 14.2
  Warren Street 4.2, 4.4, 4.6
  Whitechapel High Street 1.4
Sweet, Kim 1.24
Swinton, Tilda 10.6

Tabernacle, The 11.4
Tablet **11.4**
Tannery, The 13.6
Tate Gallery, Liverpool 1.6, 8.2
Tate Gallery, Millbank 0.3, 1.10, 12.14
  see also Art Now (Tate Gallery)
Tate Gallery of Modern Art, Bankside 0.3, 5.8, 12.10, 12.16, 13.8
Taylor, Timothy 8.6
Theis and Khan Architects 4.6
30 Underwood Street **2.14**
Thorp, David 14.8
303 gallery (New York) 13.10
Timothy Taylor Gallery **8.6**
Todd Gallery **11.2**
Townsend, Charles Harrison 1.2
Turner Prize 1.12, 1.16, 1.26, 1.28, 1.30, 4.2, 5.2, 5.10, 5.20, 7.2, 10.8, 10.10, 13.12

Vaughan, Philip 13.4
Victoria Miro Gallery 0.1, **5.2–5.4**, 13.10

Index

Waddington, Leslie 5.8
Waddington Galleries 0.1, **5.8–5.10**, 8.6
Watkins, Jonathan 2.6
Weaver, Ben 11.4
Whitechapel Art Gallery **1.2–1.4**, 5.2, 7.10
White Cube **12.2–12.4**, 12.6
Whitehouse, Mary 12.8
Wilkinson, Anthony 1.28
Wombell, Paul 7.10

index of artists

Index of Artists

Abts, Tomma 4.8
Ackerman, Chantal 7.4
Ackermann, Rita 1.30
Ackling, Roger 6.10
Adler, Amy 5.12
Aitchison, Craigie 8.6
Aitken, Doug 7.10
Allen, Phil 1.22
Almond, Darren 12.2
Altenburger, Stefan 3.4
Althoff, Kai 4.2
Anderson, Laurie 12.8
Andersson, Roger 5.16
Andre, Carl 10.10
Areen, Rasheed 10.4
Arnold, Liz 1.22, 4.10
Arrowsmith, Sue 5.12
Art & Language 1.20
Avery, Charles 5.12

B, Beth 8.2
Bacon, Francis 12.8, 13.2
Balka, Miroslaw 7.6
Balkenhol, Stephan 5.20
Banner, Fiona 12.16
Barcelo, Miquel 8.6
Barlow, Phyllida 14.12
Barney, Matthew 12.14
Beattie, Basil 13.8
Beaumes, Frederic 8.2
Becher, Bernd and Hilla 9.8
Bedia, Jose 8.6
Begg, Torie 1.8
Belton, Kate 1.6
Bening, Sadie 2.6

Best, Anna 14.4
Beuys, Joseph 6.2
Bevan, Tony 1.12, 1.32, 5.6
Billingham, Richard 7.12
Blume, Anna and Bernhard 10.2
Bob and Roberta Smith see Brill, Patrick
Boltanski, Christian 6.2
Bond, Henry 12.6
Borland, Christine 10.10
Bornstein, Jennifer 4.8
Bourgeois, Louise 6.2
Breede, Mona 10.2
Brill, Patrick 1.18
Brooks, Jason 5.12
Brown, Don 8.8
Brown, Glenn 1.22
Bruton, Jo 14.2
Buchanan, Roderick 4.10
Bulloch, Angela 1.30, 2.6, 4.2
Burden, Chris 7.8
Burgin, Victor 1.20
Butler, Ken 10.14

Cadieux, Geneviéve 12.14
Caeseberg 10.2
Calle, Sophie 12.14–12.16
Callery, Simon 1.28
Cannon, Mark 4.6
Cantor, Ellen 14.8
Cape, Francis 1.24
Carnegie, Gillian 9.10
Cartier-Bresson, Henri 13.2
Casebere, James 8.2
Catling, Brian 14.8
Chadwick, Helen 1.30

Index of Artists

Chapman, Jake and Dinos 5.2, 5.16, 8.8, 9.2, 12.10, 14.16
Chapman, Rachel 1.8
Chia, Sandro 9.4
Chilver, John 2.4
Christo 6.10
Close, Chuck 5.12
Clough, Prunella 9.10
Cohen, Bernard 1.32
Collishaw, Mat 0.3, 9.10, 10.12, 14.8
Coombs, Daniel 1.4
Coplans, John 7.6
Counsell, Melanie 1.12
Coventry, Keith 14.4
Cox, Stephen 5.6
Cragg, Tony 10.10
Craig-Martin, Michael 2.4, 5.8
Crotty, Russell 14.10
Cuddihy, Mikey 14.4
Cummings, Neil 10.14
Currin, John 8.8, 12.10

Dalwood, Dexter 12.10
Damien 0.0
Davenport, Ian 0.0, 0.2, 5.10
Davies, Kate 14.6
Davies, Peter 1.22, 12.10
Davis, Peter 4.6
Dawson, Gordon 14.12
Dawson, Ian 14.16
de Goede, Leo 1.6
de Kooning, Willem 6.2
de la Cruz, Angela 1.28, 3.4
de Souza, Bea 2.10
Deacon, Richard 10.10

Dean, Mark 8.2
Dean, Tacita 7.2
Demand, Thomas 13.10
Di Benedetto, Steve 8.2
Dickinson Rod 1.20
Dieroff, Xenia 1.12
Dieu, Sacha 8.2
Dijkstra, Rineke 7.10
Dines, Naomi 10.14
Doherty, Willie 1.12
Doig, Peter 1.2, 1.22, 5.2, 13.4
Donegan, Cheryl 8.2
Dowson, Steve 4.8
Doyle, Morgan 10.16
Dubuffet, John 5.8
Dunham, Caroll 12.4
Duvet Brothers 2.6

Edelson, Mary Beth 2.10
Edmondson, Machiko 1.8, 8.2
Eisenman, Nicole 8.2
Eisenmann, Markus 10.14
Ellis, Peter 1.28
Elson, Stephen 2.14
Elwes, Damian 10.14
Emin, Tracey 8.2, 12.2, 14.2, 14.8
English, Simon 8.2
Erlbruch, Wolf 10.2
Ernst, Max 5.8
Evans, Cerith Wyn 5.18

Fagen, Graham 1.14
Fairhurst, Angus 8.8
Fairnington, Mark 11.2
Faithfull, Simon 1.18

art london: a guide to contemporary art spaces

Falconer, David 8.8
Farquhar, Keith 6.8
Fenton, Max 1.20
Fierro, Michelle 7.6
Fleury, Sylvie 3.2, 14.8
Floyer, Ceal 1.26
Fox, Jason 14.8
Frankland, John 1.8, 14.16
Friedrich, Caspar David 4.10
Fringer, Ron 7.10
Frize, Bernard 1.16, 3.4, 7.2
Frost, Terry 1.32
Fulton, Hamish 6.12
Funakoshi, Katsura 6.10

Gabo, Naum 6.10
Galan, Julio 8.6
Gallaccio, Anya 5.20, 10.4, 13.10–13.12
Gallace, Maureen 13.10
Gallagher, Ellen 6.4
Garcia, Milo 8.2
General Idea 9.8
Genoves, Ana 13.6
Gertsch, Franz 5.6
Gilbert and George 6.2, 14.8
Gillick, Liam 4.2, 10.12
Goldberg, Neil 14.6
Goldsworthy, Andy 2.10
Gontarski, Steven 3.2, 9.6
Gonzalez-Foerster, Dominique 4.2
Gordon, Douglas 10.10, 14.6
Gormley, Anthony 12.2
Graham, Dan 10.10
Graham, Paul 12.14
Griffiths, Brian Cyril 9.6

Grimonprez, Johan 6.4
Gunning, Lucy 10.12
Gursky, Andreas 7.12, 9.4
Gussin, Graham 4.10

Hamilton, Richard 1.4
Hamilton-Finlay, Ian 10.6
Hanson, Duane 9.4
Hapaska, Siobhan 5.12, 5.14, 12.10
Harding, Alexis 8.2
Harris, Jane 14.2
Hatoum, Mona 12.2, 13.4
Hays, Dan 3.2
Heath, Claude 1.6, 14.16
Hepworth, Barbara 5.16–5.18
Heron, Patrick 9.10
Hicks, Nicola 1.32
Higgs, Matthew 1.22
Hilliard, John 1.20
Hilton, Jane 2.12
Hirst, Damien 0.0, 9.2, 9.4, 9.10, 12.2, 12.10, 14.8
Hoberman, Nicky 5.12
Hobermann, Nicky 1.8
Hoch, Matthias 10.2
Hockney, David 6.10
Höfer, Candida 4.2
Holler, Carsten 9.10
Holzer, Jenny 1.30
Hopkins, Louise 3.4
Horsfield, Craigie 7.2
Housewatch (collective) 2.8
Howson, Peter 1.32
Hughes, Des 11.4

Index of Artists

Hume, Gary 0.0, 3.2, 9.2, 12.10

Innes, Callum 7.2
Irvine, Albert 1.32
Irvine, Jaki 1.28, 7.2
Isermann, Jim 4.4

Jarman, Derek 10.10, 12.8
Jones, Gareth 4.8
Jones, Sarah 1.30, 14.16
Jones, Zebedee 5.8, 5.10, 13.4
Joseph-Lester, Jaspar 5.16
Judd, Ben 2.4
Judd, Donald 10.10, 10.12

Kapoor, Anish 10.10, 13.2
Katz, Alex 9.4
Kawamata, Tadashi 6.10, 10.4
Kay, Emma 12.10
Kelly, Mary 12.8
Kentridge, William 5.22
Kessler, Rob 14.12
Ketter, Clay 12.4
Kiefer, Anselm 6.2, 14.8
Kilimnik, Karen 12.2, 12.6
Kippenberger, Martin 7.8
Koons, Jeff 6.2
Kosuth, Joseph 9.10
Kovats, Tania 5.16–5.18, 13.4
Krisanamis, Udomsak 5.2, 14.10

Lalic, Maria 11.2
Landers, Sean 11.4, 12.4
Landy, Michael 5.10
Lane, Abigail 5.2, 9.10

Lasker, Jonathan 8.6, 13.4
Leapman, David 14.16
Leapman, Edwina 6.10, 13.8
Leger, Fernand 5.8
Lewandowska, Marysia 10.14
Lewis, Simon 11.2
LeWitt, Sol 9.2
Lewitt, Sol 10.10
Long, Charles 7.6
Long, Richard 2.10
Lowe, Rachel 7.10
Lowe, Robin 5.4
Lucas, Sarah 0.3, 8.8, 9.2, 12.2

McCail, Chad 14.2
McCarthy, Paul 13.6
McCollum, Allan 10.4
Macgill, Elizabeth 3.4
McGinn, Martin 14.16
Maloney, Martin 6.2, 9.6, 12.10
Manzoni, Piero 10.6
Marchan, Javier 3.4
Martin, Jason 10.12
Maslin, Steven 3.2
Matisse, Henri 5.8
Merz, Gerhard 6.6
Metzger, Gustave 2.14
Miller, Neil 2.14
Milroy, Lisa 1.16
Minter, Marilyn 3.2
Minton, John 1.4
Miro, Joan 5.8
Mitchell, Matt 2.14
Moffatt, Tracey 1.8, 5.4
Mondrian, Piet 6.10

Moores, James 10.14
Mori, Mariko 10.6, 13.6, 14.8
Morrison, Paul 2.4
Moszynski, Andrew 14.2
Mucck, Ron 1.32
Muehl, Otto 2.14
Muller, Christopher 10.2

Nauman, Bruce 9.2, 13.2
Nelson, Mike 9.8
Neudecker, Mariele 4.10, 10.14
Newman, Avis 1.12, 10.12
Nicholson, Ben 5.8, 6.10
Niemis, Renato 14.12
Nitsch, Hermann 2.14
Noble, Paul 1.30, 12.10, 14.8
Noble, Tim 2.2, 2.12, 10.12

O' Brien, Dermot 14.12
Oates, Daniel 8.10
Ocampo, Manuel 13.12
Ofili, Chris 1.28, 3.2, 5.2, 9.2, 10.8, 13.8, 14.8
Ono, Yoko 10.10
Oppenheim, Meret 12.10
Orimoto, Tatsumi 2.14
Orridge, Genesis P 12.8
Owen, Justin 1.20
Owens, Laura 8.8

Pacheho, Ana Maria 1.32
Palmer, Kate 1.34
Pareno, Philippe 13.8
Parker, Cornelia 1.16, 7.2, 10.6
Parsons, Jonathan 14.6

Patterson, Richard 6.4, 13.4
Patterson, Simon 10.10, 14.6
Pearlstein, Alix 3.2
Pearson, Cath 4.6
Periton, Simon 8.10
Perkins, Gary 1.6
Pernice, Manfred 5.16
Pessoli, Alessandro 4.8
Peyton, Elizabeth 8.8
Pflumm, Daniel 5.16
Phaophanit, Vong 5.20
Phillips, Richard 5.22
Picasso, Pablo 12.8
Piggot, Hadrian 13.4
Pimlott, Mark 11.2
Pittman, Lari 4.8
Polke, Sigmar 6.2
Pommerer, Peter 12.6

Quay, The Brothers 12.8
Quinn, Marc 12.14, 14.8
Quinton, Neill 14.4

Rae, Fiona 0.0, 0.2, 5.10, 9.2
Raedecker, Michael 12.10
Raho, Alessandro 1.6
Rayson, David 1.30
Reed, David 3.4
Reinhardt, Ad 9.10
Richter, Gerhard 2.4, 6.2, 10.2
Ricketts, Sophy 9.10
Rielly, James 8.2–8.4
Riley, Bridget 2.4
Rio Branco, Miguel 7.6
Rist, Pipilotti 1.16

Rockman, Alexis 7.6
Rodchenko, Alexander 6.10
Rolph, Donny 14.2
Roth, Dieter 10.2
Rovner, Michal 12.14
Ruscha, Ed 6.2
Ryman, Robert 3.4, 10.10

Saville, Jenny 1.32, 14.2
Schlieker, Andrea 10.4
Schnabel, Julian 8.6
Schumann, Christian 12.4
Schütte, Thomas 1.2, 9.4
Scully, Sean 8.6
Shiraishi, Yuko 6.10
Shonibare, Yinka 5.20, 11.4
Sighicelli, Elisa 14.2
Simmonds, Gary 1.4
Simpson, D J 2.4
Simpson, Jane 1.22, 5.16
Smith, Edward 6.2
Smith, Ray 8.6
Smith, Terry 14.12
Snell, Rosie 1.34
Sokurov, Alexander 7.2
Solano, Susana 6.6
Spero, Nancy 6.6
Stahl, Andrew 1.32
Stapleton, Fergal 2.10, 10.14
Starling, Simon 1.26
Starr, Georgina 6.6–6.8, 12.14, 13.6, 14.8
Staton, Sarah 4.6, 14.6
Stepanek, Alice, and Steven Maslin 3.2
Stewart, Kerry 1.22, 5.20
Stewart, Nathaniel 14.12

Stewart, Stephanie 6.2
Stezaker, John 1.20, 14.2
Still, Clyfford 1.6
Stockholder, Jessica 12.4, 13.4
Streuli, Beat 12.14
Strindberg, Madeleine 1.4, 13.8
Stubbs, Mike 4.6
Sturgis, Daniel 1.22, 3.2
Sugimoto, Hiroshi 5.6
Svankmajer, Jan 12.8

Takahashi, Tomoko 9.6, 11.4, 14.4, 14.16
Taylor, Marcus 8.2
Taylor, Stuart 3.4
Taylor-Wood, Sam 1.16, 1.26, 5.16
Thorpe, David 5.20
Tillmans, Wolfgang 1.30
Timoney, Padraig 3.2
Titchner, Mark 1.6
Torres, Felix Gonzalez 9.10
Trockel, Rosemary 1.4
Turk, Gavin 8.2, 9.2, 12.2, 14.10
Turrell, James 5.6
Tutti, Cosey Fanni 12.8

Uklanski, Piotr 12.10
Ulay and Abramovic 6.4
Uslé, Juan 8.6

Vallance, Jeffrey 14.8
van der Stokker, Lily 14.10
Viner, Darrell 2.6
Viola, Bill 1.2, 14.8
von Weiler, Carl 14.12

art london: a guide to contemporary art spaces

Index of Artists

Voorsanger, Jessica 1.28

Wall, Jeff 1.2
Wallinger, Mark 0.3, 2.6, 6.6, 8.2, 9.2, 13.10, 13.12
Waplington, Nick 2.16
Warhol, Andy 6.2, 9.2
Warren, Rebecca 2.10, 10.14
Wearing, Gillian 0.3, 1.16, 1.30, 2.6, 9.10
Webster, Sue 2.2, 2.12
Wentworth, Richard 10.10
White, Pae 4.8
Whiteread, Rachel 1.16, 6.2, 9.2, 9.4
Williams, Sue 8.8
Williamson, Erlend 2.10
Wilson, Jane and Louise 2.6, 2.8, 14.6
Wilson, Keith 14.16
Wilson, Richard 1.10–1.12
Winters, Terry 1.4, 12.4
Wood, Lucy 1.8
Wright, Elizabeth 1.24, 2.6

Yokomizo, Shizuka 4.6
Yuskavage, Lisa 4.8

Zittel, Andren 8.10

also available from ellipsis

Ellipsis London Guides

london: a guide to recent architecture

Samantha Hardingham

A snapshot of London, with a wave of Lottery-funded projects and the Jubilee Line Extension designed by the UK's most exciting architects, while the Millennium Dome provides a controversial full stop to the century.

ISBN 1 899858 92 X

eat london: architecture and eating

Samantha Hardingham

An updated edition of the best-selling guide to London's flourishing restaurant scene. This book describes a key factor in the success or failure or any restaurant – its design.

ISBN 1 84166 003 5

dyke london: a guide

Rosa Ainley

Clubs come and go, homosexuality goes in and out of style, but the life of the London dyke continues. This guide suggests venues to tempt every-dyke, whatever level of (in)visibility you might crave, not ignoring the daily necessities – buying underwear, furniture, food, or make-up.

ISBN 1 899858 74 1

gay london: a guide

William McLoughlin *et al*

Much more than a mere listing, this guide provides an insight into how a gay man might enjoy the more esoteric pleasures the city has to offer, from the pursuit of spectral figures in Abney Park Cemetery to contemplation of exactly what form the muse took that inspired Frederic Lord Leighton when building his house in Holland Park.

ISBN 1 899858 73 3

PRICE £8.00

Samantha Hardingham

London

A guide to recent architecture

•••

samantha hardingham

eat london

architecture eating and drinking

•••

rose sinley

dyke london

a guide

•••

jones, mclaughlin, martin, wyllie

gay london

a guide

•••

•••

The Folded Lie

Opening in Tokyo with the trial of 28 Japanese leaders accused of war crimes, and closing with John Major's indictment on similar charges relating to the Gulf War, *The Folded Lie* questions the world system of war and peace. The intriguing story of Willem Boymans, a fascinating and at times irritating character, is bounded by a prologue focusing on the anti-war Article Nine of the Japanese constitution and an epilogue observing the late '90s modern-art scene into the millennium. Willem devotes his life to undoing 'the folded lie' (W H Auden) of war and, driven by anger and guilt over his own wartime role, commits himself to the pursuit of enforceable world law to criminalise 'state belligerency'.

The Folded Lie offers a complex mixture of the real and the fictional, the local and the global, including the multiple happenings of the Millennium Art Show at Bankside, the public and private lives of a Japanese defense attorney in suburban Tokyo, the cultural conflicts of east and west, taking in Christmas Humphreys, Greenpeace, Stockhausen and Joshua Compston along the way.

ISBN 1 899858 54 7
PRICE £18.00

Jeremy Cooper

Mekons United

The Mekons were one of a group of bands to emerge from Leeds University art school in the late 1970s (others included The Three Johns and the Gang of Four). The band has moved from punk through various musical styles, worked with dancers, artists and writers, and produced a string of albums. Unlike most of the bands who formed in the wake of the Sex Pistols, the Mekons have never stopped developing, and their work has remained deeply rooted in a politically inspired art practice. Recent Mekon activities include an installation with American performance artist Vito Acconci and *Pussy, King of the Pirates*, a collaboration with Kathy Acker.

This book – a necessary publication for all Mekons fans and anyone interested in the relationship between art and popular culture – presents a selection of Mekons art, and includes a major essay by Terry Atkinson on the pop-art explosion and the politics that led eventually to punk, essays on the economics of rock 'n' roll, the topography of Leeds, football and popular culture, art theory, and on the Mekons themselves by Greil Marcus. The book also includes extracts from 'Living in Sin', the Mekons' novel in progress, with contributions from Kathy Acker, and the *Mekons United* CD with more than an hour of music.

ISBN 1 899858 19 9
PRICE £24.95

Terry Atkinson and others

K Foundation Burn a Million Quid

In the early hours of the 23 August 1994, in a boathouse on Jura, off the west coast of Scotland, the trustees of the K Foundation, Jimmy Cauty and Bill Drummond, burned the assets of the foundation – £1 million in £50 notes. The money was the result of Cauty and Drummond's enormously successful ventures in pop music, first as the Justified Ancients of Mu Mu (the JAMS), then as the Timelords, and latterly as one of the most successful bands of the late 1980s and early 1990s, the KLF. After disbanding the KLF in 1992 Cauty and Drummond set up the K Foundation. Their best-known foray into the art world was the presentation of £40,000 to Rachel Whiteread for the worst body of art of 1993. Whiteread had been awarded the £20,000 Turner Prize a few days earlier.

The burning of the £1 million was filmed and a year after the event Cauty and Drummond returned to Jura to show the people of the island the film (*Watch the K Foundation Burn a Million Quid*) and to inaugurate a series of screenings and discussions held in various locations – all in an attempt to understand just what the K Foundation had done.

Was it art?

What was the morality of the burning?

Was it a publicity stunt?

What should they do next?

This book is a further exploration of the act.

ISBN 1 899858 37 7
PRICE £15.00

Chris Brook and Gimpo